James Scarth Gale

Korean Sketches

James Scarth Gale
Korean Sketches
ISBN/EAN: 9783337014292

Printed in Europe, USA, Canada, Australia, Japan

Cover: Foto ©ninafisch / pixelio.de

More available books at **www.hansebooks.com**

KOREAN SKETCHES

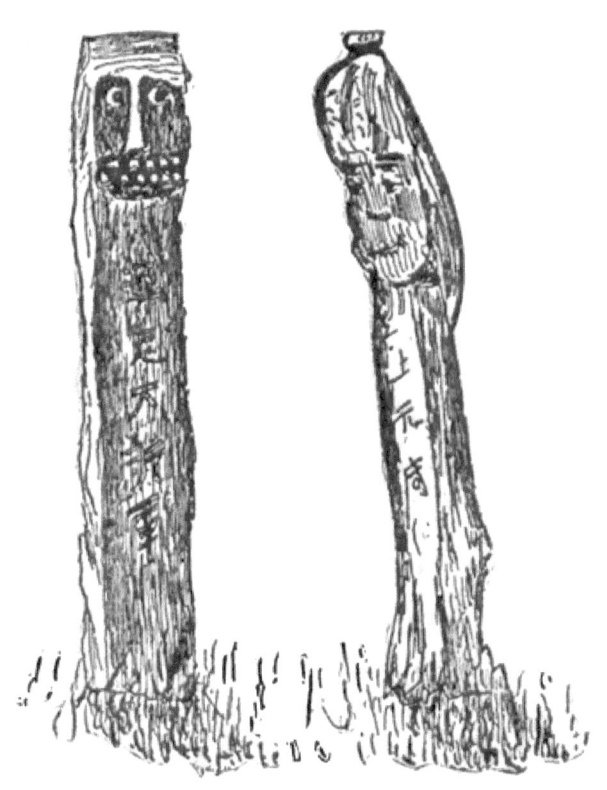

DEVIL POSTS.

SEOUL.

KOREAN SKETCHES

BY
Rev. James S. Gale, B.A.
(*Toronto University*)
Of the American Presbyterian Mission, Wŭnsan, Korea

Chicago New York Toronto
Fleming H. Revell Company

Preface

COMPARATIVELY little has as yet been written that gives an idea of Korean life and character. After some nine years of intimate association with this quaintest and oldest of living races, I have put these sketches together, believing that they give a correct picture of the Hermit people as it is, and as it has been since the long forgotten days before our Anglo-Saxon race came into existence. May they be instrumental in drawing young men and women into deeper sympathy with our brothers and sisters of the Hermit Kingdom!

JAMES S. GALE.

WŎNSAN, KOREA.

ON LIFE.

Ye white gull of the sea
    So free!
What earthly care or rue,
Is there for a bird like you,
Swimming on the sea?
    Tell of those happy islands where
    Poor mortals may resign their care,
And follow after thee!

Contents

CHAP.		PAGE
I.	FIRST IMPRESSIONS	11
II.	THE COOLIE	52
III.	THE YALU AND BEYOND	72
IV.	FROM POVERTY TO RICHES	104
V.	THE KOREAN PONY	117
VI.	ACROSS KOREA	127
VII.	THE KOREAN BOY	143
VIII.	KOREAN NEW YEAR	157
IX.	THE KOREAN MIND	174
X.	THE KOREAN GENTLEMAN	182
XI.	KOREA'S PRESENT CONDITION	194
XII.	SOME SPECIAL FRIENDS	222
XIII.	A MISSIONARY CHAPTER	238
XIV.	METHODIST EPISCOPAL CHURCH SOUTH IN KOREA	257

ON LIFE.

More than half of life is over.
Young again? no, never! never!
Cease, then, from this growing gray,
And as you are, so please to stay;
These white hairs must surely know
How to turn more slowly so!

PHILOSOPHICAL.

This mountain green, these waters blue,
They were not made, they simply grew;
And 'tween the hills and waters here,
I, too, have grown as I appear.
Youth grows, until the years unfold,
Then age comes on by growing old.

ALL AT ONE SHOVEL

LIST OF ILLUSTRATIONS

SEOUL		*Frontispiece*
DEVIL POSTS		Page 2
ALL AT ONE SHOVEL		" 9
SOME OF THE INHABITANTS } THE HOPE OF THE NATION }	*Facing*	" 40
THE COOLIE } THE COOLIE'S WIFE }	"	" 52
THE KOREAN PONY	"	" 118
THE CANGUE } ACCORDING TO LAW }	"	" 170
THE WARDROBE OF THE GENTRY } KÖSIKI (WHAT-YOU-MAY-CALL-HER) }	"	" 190
WŎNSAN JAPANESE SETTLEMENT } WŎNSAN CHINESE SETTLEMENT }	"	" 200
H. H. PRINCE EUI WHA } KOREAN MINISTER TO THE UNITED STATES }	"	" 222
BUDDHIST MONKS } BUDDHIST PAGODA }	"	" 234

A KOREAN LOVE SONG.

That rock heaved up on yonder shore,
I'll chisel out and cut and score,
And mark the hair, and make the horns,
And put on feet, and all the turns
    Required for a cow;
And then, my love, if you go 'way,
I'll saddle up my bovine gray,
    And follow you somehow.

KOREAN FILIAL PIETY.

That pond'rous weighted iron bar
I'll spin out thin in threads so far
To reach the sun, and fasten on
And tie him in before he's gone,
That parents who are growing gray
May not get old another day.

Korean Sketches

I

FIRST IMPRESSIONS

KOREA, as doubtless you know, is a peninsula stretching southwards, in a position to form a convenient highway for the Japanese, when on their way to the Celestial Empire. It is supposed to contain a population of twelve millions; I say supposed, as the census returns are anything but accurate. The area is about the same as that of the state of Utah. The configuration of the land consists of a succession of mountain ranges so that, when travelling, you are kept on a constant tiptoe of expectation, each pass revealing vistas beyond. Koreans have an expression that is frequently repeated: *San way you san san pool chin* (over the hills, hills again, hills without number). In 1890, on a journey through the south, I called on the governor of Kyüng-sang, the largest province of the kingdom; and one of his first questions was, "Do the mountains sit as close together in your honorable country?" These mountains form sites for ancestral graves, are looked upon as dragons, and, as the native says, distribute various atmospheres over the land, propitious and unpropitious.

The following spring, the same governor was called upon to decide a dispute that arose concerning one of these dragon elevations, and as his decision gave dissatisfaction, he was given a dose of poison in a watermelon a week or two later; so the grave dispute was settled. You may maltreat Koreans with impunity, in fact a traveller may take possession of their rooms, and turn them out on the street, and they will take it as nothing serious, if not a joke; but touch an ancestral grave and your life will pay for it.

The people of Korea claim to be a race descended from the gods, slightly admixed with Chinese; no wonder they develop at times extraordinary traits.

They have had a horror of foreigners, *yang-in*, or men of the sea, from time immemorial. Weather-worn tablets still stand by the roadside, in essence, marked thus: "If you meet a foreigner kill him; he who lets him go by is a traitor to his country." It speaks well for Korea that she could lay by these murderous traditions in a day, and bear with foreigners as she has since the signing of the treaties. It is ten years and more since the "barbarian" entered, ten years of political chaos it has been,

First Impressions

and yet no European or American has been injured, or threatened, or treated in any other than the kindest way.

Missionary work has gone on unmolested, and there are a thousand and more Christians, having many established places for regular worship.

Amongst my first impressions, I recall being quite overwhelmed by the wide pantaloons and white dress of a Korean, who came on board ship in Nagasaki harbor on my first arrival there. Why such a dress, and wherefore the topknot? Little did I dream that he valued his topknot so highly, or that in every seam of his wide pantaloons were stitched ancestral reverence, Confucian propriety, ancient traditions, and other tremendous considerations that certainly required all that width of garment, and more too, could piece goods as wide as the wearer's aspirations be obtained.

Our ship came to anchor in Fusan bay, which has but two narrow openings and from the anchorage appears landlocked. At the main entrance are immense sentinel cliffs that stand guard looking seaward. In the year 1893, one pleasant June evening, we were just making the harbor through this entrance, when suddenly the gong sounded to reverse engines, and all passengers made for the deck. The chief officer was ordering a boat to be lowered almost at the point of his revolver, as though life depended upon it, while the captain on the bridge was using strong English. What such a commotion could mean we were entirely at a loss to know, until word was passed, that a man was overboard. After ten minutes searching, we saw them fish up a drowning Chinaman, who, it seemed, in a mad freak, had jumped overboard. My wife remarked to a Russian lady passenger standing by, "Too bad about the poor Chinaman." "Humph!" said the Russian lady with a shrug of her shoulders, "Plenty Chinaman!"

But I am digressing; on this first trip, when the ship dropped anchor, we were in full view of the brown denuded hills which look so uninviting in the chill December atmosphere. A passenger friend and I went ashore, and found on the landing a group of well-dressed natives wearing horsehair hats with ribbons tied under the chin. They had their hands buried far up in their wide sleeves, and stood immovable as a group of Buddhas. We set out on a walk for the town, a mile or so distant, and the natives began to move after us. They were an uncanny looking lot, so many seemed to wear an expression of sore eyes and smallpox. The dogs, too, seemed all to have the mange. As soon as possible we sought refuge from such company and went on board ship.

Our voyage of more than four hundred miles from Fusan to Chemulpo was among rocks, and along a dangerous, partially surveyed seacoast. A deal of faith is required to sail here, with not a single beacon fire or light to assist the navigator. Many a time since I have crossed this same sea, but never without a feeling of expectancy, as we passed in the darkness black banks of solid rock just visible above the water. One steamer with some of my own acquaintances and friends on board, struck and went down here. This wreck has left a solemn spot in the grim rocky sea. The wonder is we have not more of us sounded in person its yellow depths.

At Chemulpo, where the tide rises about thirty feet, an immense sea rolls in and out twice a day. When it is in, it laps the foot of the cliffs and mountains along the coast line; when it is out, miles of mud are seen, where crabs and turtles and octopus play leap-frog and pull-a-way together.

At last we reached Seoul, through a journey and into surroundings as mysterious as dreamland. Viewed as a whole, Seoul is said to be the most picturesque city in the East; viewed in detail, it contains much to make one shudder: but the people are kind, and entirely different from the cruel race I had thought them to be. I cannot however omit to mention this objec-

tionable custom which prevails more or less
throughout all the East, and which is so horrifying to a newcomer, namely, the constant
presence of the dead. Kindly and sorrowfully
we bury our dead out of sight in the hope of a
resurrection and meeting hereafter; but not so
the Korean; he ties his dead in a mat and leaves
him to bake and fester in the sun. The very
atmosphere is tainted, and one becomes an expert in distinguishing the noxious odors of
smallpox and cholera victims from the ordinary
smells of the far East. This subject reminds
me of a beautiful landscape overlooking the sea
at Fusan, which my Korean friend and I were
enjoying one glorious afternoon, when we happened suddenly upon a dead child, horrible in
decay, planted on four bamboo poles. The
river Styx is nothing to the sights and smells
past which Confucius leads you on his way to
heaven. Shortly after my arrival, while taking a walk outside of the little east gate of the
capital, I saw a hundred and more of these objects covered with matting. "What are they?"
I asked. "Those are the dead." "The dead?
Why don't you bury them?" "Cannot; you
must first find a propitious site, otherwise burial
will bring ruin to the family." A day or so
later, two of us were riding on horseback along
the main road to the east of the city, when suddenly my horse gave a start, and there I beheld

three decapitated bodies, with heads lying on the roadway. I returned home in disgust, feeling that I would like to get out of this country with its horrible dead ; but time works wonders. I began to see another side—that the people loved these things as little as I—that it was a part of their Confucian religion—and that they needed the real Light of Life so much the more.

In March, 1889, I decided to make my first venture inland. Foreigners had travelled through the country, but no one had as yet attempted to take up his residence outside of the capital. The element of uncertainty, which adds interest to any undertaking, helped me. I sent seventy dollars by a trusty native with which to buy me a house in Häju, the capital of Whang-hä (Yellow sea) province. He returned with the money three weeks later as though the furies had been after him. The good citizens of Häju had heard that he was the emissary of a "barbarian," and so had rid their town of him forthwith. No foreign residence yet defiles the precincts of the sacred city of Häju. In spite of this act of defiance on the part of these good people, I felt that I would have to go, even though no house awaited me. With a horse or two, a soldier, a boy and a stableman, I bade my friends good-bye, and turned toward Häju, sending a letter ahead to a Mr. An living in Chang-yön, some distance beyond, who was recommended to me as honest.

The soldier who accompanied me had a very red nose and a most fragrant atmosphere that smacked of *sul* (rice whiskey). He was evidently "up" in the arts of peace, quite as much as in the arts of war. He would jog along at a peculiar trot just in front of my pony until he saw a party coming, when at once his manner would become animated. He would shout his commands to clear the way, dismount, stop smoking, and attack them like a perfect whirlwind. They in every case bore with abject submission to be kicked and cuffed. The first opportunity I called him, and said I would have to have this stopped, that I never could consent to go through the country like a brigand, and that he would have to put a check on the exercise of his authority. He, however, explained that his was good Korean custom, and that if I did not go through the country with some degree of form, I never would be respected. I found later that the only way to escape this proper form, was to dismiss the soldier and travel in the company of a civilian.

On leaving the capital, as I discovered later, the rascal had asked the magistrate of each district to send word ahead to the next official town, that the "great man" was coming. Who the "great man" was, or in what capacity he was travelling, never once was raised, but every effort was made to show respect. Just as soon as a company of district runners left me others were on the way to act as escort. My passport was sufficient to call forth every attention, and the pretended humility of the people along this first trip inland was quite embarrassing. To feel at the same time that I had repaid civility with abuse, was painful, ignorant as I was of good Korean custom.

Once night overtook us while still seven miles from our destination. The soldier kept well ahead shouting over his shoulder "push on!" The little lad of fifteen years who had charge of my pony, had already run thirty-three miles over the gummy roads proving his powers of endurance. We crossed a ferry, and night rolled over us dark, and cold, and clammy. Now every voice echoed as we rode along. The horses were wearied, as was I, sitting since daylight in the cramped position in the saddle. But round and round we went, over hills skirting low woodlands, picking our way through the marshy rice fields where groups of white wild fowl stood like snowbanks in the mud. Peculiar calls there were. "What are those?" I asked. "*Puhöngi*," said he. "But what are *puhöngi?*" "The bird with the big round eyes," said the boy. Along with these sounds, over every distant hamlet arose a white cloud of smoke, announcing fire for the evening meal.

When so dark that we could no longer proceed, we came to a halt before a small thatched hut, and here my soldier stood kicking and pounding the door ready to break it in. At last it was opened, and I saw him cuff the owner of the place and order him out at once. After a succession of Nei-i-i-s (yes), long drawn out, the proprietor came forth carrying a stiff narrow twist of straw, some ten feet in length. He lit one end, and then we saw what it meant. With this as torch he led the way. The sparks flew into my eyes and over me in showers. Every few minutes he would break off the burned ends by poking it against the ground and then swing it to make it burn afresh. When we came to another hamlet, the first torch-bearer, who had been pressed into service, returned home leaving some one in this neighborhood to take his place. This last part of the seven miles was accomplished at a run, the soldier whipping up the torch-bearer when he lagged. With hurrahs and calls of various kinds, we went sweeping into our destination, the inhabitants peeking out of the partially opened door or window to see what manner of official could be passing in such state and with such variety of clatter and call.

The marks of respect shown me through the indefatigable efforts of my soldier, increased to such an extent that, when a week later I entered the city of Hăju, a large portion of the population came out to meet me. The morning of that day had been exceedingly peaceful, the larks singing overhead, and the spring atmosphere softening the view on every hand; but it was the peace that presages turmoil, for by noon, when still twelve miles from the city, horses and men dressed in colors civil and military, were waiting to do me honor. There was no opportunity to decline these favors, so I received them boldly and made the best of them. A certain satisfaction in the irony of fate possessed me, when I beheld the defiant citizens of Hăju, who had refused to sell me a house, kicked and tumbled by my incorrigible soldier, while I rode into the governor's *yamen* in proper Korean form.

I remained in Hăju two weeks, and several times was ushered into the presence of the governor, a nervous man, who seemed in a perpetual state of uneasiness. He asked my name, how old I was, if I was married, and what I had come to do in the land of Morning Calm. He wished to know my country, and when I said Mi-guk, he inquired of the servants gazing in at the window if they knew to which of the outskirts of the universe such a kingdom belonged. Of course they knew not, and the governor shook his head doubtfully.

A great wall of China seemed to separate us. My country, my calling, my appearance, were all mysteries to him. For example, why had I taken my hat off on entering, when Korean custom requires you to put it on if you will show respect. I tried to say, that our country, being on the other side of the earth, had fallen into many customs the very opposite of those in Korea. "The other side of the earth," what did that mean? And at once we were into the perplexing question of the shape of matter in general. But, says the governor, Confucius says that the heavens are round and the earth, square and flat, and here this foreign gentleman pretends the opposite; and a shock of nervousness took him that threatened violent prostration. The wall of China grew apace, till a servant brought in a table of food, and His Excellency asked me to partake, eyeing me closely the while to see whether I ate the food or the brass bowls and chopsticks; for Koreans hold that different degrees of spiritual being require different material for food, some eat metal, some wood, some grass, some air, while the purely human eats rice, pork, raw fish, etc. The first spoonful of rice I took levelled that wall of China. The governor had unfailing proof that I was human, and he could afford to overlook minor differences on the question of the universe, seeing that we had in common this capacity for rice that made us fellow mortals.

Fifteen days of sightseeing more than sufficed to acquaint me with the characteristics of the city of Hăju. Like everything else in Korea, it speaks of a prosperity that has passed away ages before. The walls were in ruins, the huts simply heaps of mud and sticks like a beaver camp. Yet in the midst of this squalor gentlemen were moving about in immaculate silken robes. The acquaintances I made were, just as I have since found Koreans, intelligent and interesting. The mystery is, that so many bright minds can be content with so low a civilization. Their excuse is, that Confucius commended Anja for living in abject poverty, and there exemplifying the beauties of *To* (doctrine). It is certainly due in some way to the damaging influence of the Chinese classics. A company of educated natives will listen with marked indifference to any subject, interesting or uninteresting; but raise the question of the form of a Chinese character, and at once every mind is alert, as though it were a matter of importance whether you write it with two dots or four: the form of the character so often being the absorbing subject rather than the meaning conveyed by it.

One day a plain-looking countryman unexpectedly announced himself at my door, and said he was An to whose care I had been intrusted by the letter sent in advance. He asked me the ordinary questions, how old I was, was my father alive, and then proposed that we start at once for his home in Chang-yön. A day later I was jogging along on a pack pony with two runners ahead in blue coats, wide hats, and red head tassels.

Our adventures were numerous, for these runners whom the governor insisted on my taking, simply cleared the country-side of every traveller. Their calls were heard in the distance, and unfortunates who found themselves on the king's highway fled wildly. It was in vain that I remonstrated. They would bow profoundly on both hands, and the next moment would so furiously set upon a fellow countryman, who, perhaps, had ventured with pipe in mouth to look at us, that all that was left of him was a confusion of topknot and padded trousers. In one case a whole town rose in arms, but, nothing daunted, these hangmen charged the entire community and scattered them in all directions.

I was determined to be rid of them, so making them a present, liberal according to Mr. An's reckoning, said they might go. They were both prostrated in the dust and covered with confusion at this turn in affairs. The more violent runner who had but one eye, wept copiously through it, saying that he had hoped we might ever be together as he had had a better time in my service than he had ever had before. Partings are sad—but we parted.

That same day, just as evening was coming on, Mr. An and I wound our way through a high mountain pass. He warned me repeatedly of *horangi* (tigers). A neighbor of his had been carried off through this pass and eaten only a half moon before. At the summit, a rushing through the grass startled us, and there was one creature, and another, and another that went by us like a flash, six in all—not tigers—but deer. They had been feeding in the valley and were now on their way home. We breathed more freely and whipped up the ponies. It was nearly ten o'clock when we reached An's village, which was dark as Egypt, and would never have announced itself but for the dogs that smelt the foreigner and simply roared themselves into hysteria.

The room into which I was hurried had a feeble light in one corner that gasped and sputtered. The mud walls, mud ceiling, mud floor, and atmosphere of smoke that enveloped everything, reminded me of a lodging place travellers might find who were on their way to the centre of the earth, or, as the ancients called it, Hades.

The first moments were interrupted by the entrance of half a dozen natives. No subterranean dwellers could have worn a wilder appearance. They were partially dressed in what had once been white, but what was now as smoky in color as their own bodies. The hair, knotted in native style on the top, had unravelled itself over face and shoulders. One after another they squatted silently in the farther corners of the room, puffing, meanwhile, clouds of tobacco smoke. In this manner an hour or so passed.

There is a feeling of loneliness and indescribable depression that comes over one's soul when being long gazed at as a wild beast. The paper doors and windows are poked full of finger holes, and back of each a dark eye takes position and rivets you with unwinking gaze. A single eye without its companion orb or accompanying facial expression to give it meaning, exerts an uncanny influence that prompts one to blow out the light by which it sees or turn a stream of water on it. The eyes that beset one in Korea, before and behind, have proven one of the hardest trials of missionary life. This first night at friend An's was no exception, and the only way I could get rest and sleep was by consigning all to darkness.

I was disturbed by the hard matting and the heated floor, and was glad when morning came.

Breakfast was handed in through a rear doorway opening into the unexplored region where the women live. The mystery that compassed the room the previous night, had departed. Old-fashioned sunlight, so matter-of-fact, had given it chase, and now overhead and about me were the friendly forms of mud and straw and cobwebs.

The street that morning had been wild with tumult. Every now and then great sounds would explode just in front of my door. I asked my host what the war was about. "Nothing," said he, "no war," resuming his pipe.

While trying to imagine what a riot could possibly be like when peace was so noisy, I was asked to take a walk to see the town. Passing the doorway we came upon a group of coolies whose appearance neither familiarity nor sunlight could civilize. They looked just as wild as ever as they walked round me continuing the survey of the evening before. The streets of the place were narrow. Gutters cut through the clay here and there were half filled with stagnant water that charged the air with poisonous odors. The houses, as elsewhere, were low mud huts covered with straw, under the floors of which were smoking fires. The abode of Mr. An, where I slept, turned out to be a palatial residence compared with many. Every alley was thronging with men, some passing hurriedly, others grouped about smoking pipes two and three feet long. They questioned An vigorously as to who I was and where I had come from. An did his part exceedingly well,—seeing that he was getting only eight dollars a month for the safe preservation of my head, in a land, where executions are as common as "a dollar and costs or thirty days" at home.

All being satisfactory we moved on. Such a multitude of dogs and naked children I had never seen before. The children ran on first approach, but not so the dogs. With glaring eyes and bristling necks they threatened me from beneath gateways, or gathered in howling conferences behind the bamboo paling. I remarked here in my best Korean, "For mercy's sake, An, why don't you kill these dogs?" "Too early yet," An replied, "we'll kill them later on." "But why don't you kill them now and quiet the town?" I asked. "Why," he said, "you know that dogs are not good eating in spring. We wait till summer before we kill them. Do you eat them in spring in your country?" "Well, no!" I said with some surprise, "I would not like to be guilty of eating one of those at any time." "Don't you use them at all?" he asked again. "No! Not in our country." An wore a look of disgust at the thought of such fools as we must be. By noon we had again reached home after my first view of Chang-yön town.

For the three months that I remained there life was very simple. I sat day after day in one end of the room, crosslegged on the stone floor, until my ankles were calloused harder than the heel, and my knees had grown accustomed to the new feat of bending outwards. Floor life is more sociable and conducive to conversation than being perched upon chairs. I always had callers. They would come from earliest dawn and put me through the list of questions that are unconsciously asked of every traveller in the Far East: What is your family name? Where do you reside? Have you come in peace? Are your parents alive? How old are you? How many brothers to you? Have you a son? What have you come to do? Do you know where the people live who have only one eye in their head? Where is the woman's kingdom? What's your salary? Can you pull your teeth out when you like, or your eyes? Have you medicine that will cure everything?

An's father, who was a vigorous old man, used to help me through this list after he had heard it often enough to know my answers by heart. It seemed to delight him to impart such information to the passers-by. He would hail these and tell them to come inside and see a man that knew everything. "A very good man," grandfather An would say. "You can ask him anything you like and he'll answer you." Little did he know the pent-up disinclinations that were often ready to burst forth on these never-ending interviewers.

An senior always awoke me in the morning. He would spread a large mat on the ground just in front of my window, and empty beans or rice on it to dry in the morning sun. The chickens would make straight for the heap, whereupon Mr. An would shout Hu-u-u-u! Hu! at the top of his voice. The hens did not mind it, but it always awoke me.

My nights were passed on the stone floor with only a blanket between me and the hard matting. I used to dream in those days. The wooden block under my head seemed full of the spirit of night wandering, and scarcely a night passed without some gigantic effort in dreamland. The food, perhaps, was partly responsible, it being only rice and weeds pickled in salt water. Sometimes I had an egg when the unseen Mrs. An could capture it for me.

Eggs have peculiar ways in Korea. A much respected American friend of mine eats eggs when he travels, and plays the guitar at times to vary the monotony of life. One evening, while on a country tour, he arrived in an out-of-the-way town. Placing his guitar in a safe corner by itself he sat waiting for the

First Impressions

evening meal. He asked the host to cook an egg or two with his rice. "Ah!" said the host, "but there are no eggs in town. May I die and may the worms eat me if there is an egg to be had in all these quarters:" and the patient sojourner had to content himself with rice and plain weed steeped in salt water. When supper was over the people of the town gathered in, and one of the first questions was, "What is the instrument over in that corner?" "That's what I play on when I sing." "Would the great man please play some now?" every one asked at once. "I might," said he, "but then I have had no eggs for supper, and so have no heart to play." "But there are not any eggs." "Neither is there any music." "*Kulsai!*" A few minutes later a dozen as nice fresh eggs as ever gladdened his heart were laid at his feet, with the respectful request, "Will the great man please play?" The host was there too and enjoyed the music, in full view of the eggs that were spread out before him.

We had a wedding while I was there, the bridegroom being An senior. His wife had died some years before, and now he was to marry again. An junior said of all unparalleled pieces of folly dad's marrying again was the most foolish. But Korea permits of no remonstrance on the part of children, so the wedding came off smoothly. The bride was brought in a closed chair, and ushered into the inner quarters with bustle and call indicative of rank and importance. Though a young girl, she became mother-in-law to an elderly woman, who was the wife of An junior, and trouble began. The Eastern Question is nothing compared with the entanglements henceforth in the house of An. Hanp'yŏng, who was An junior, came to me one night and said he thought he would die. He said his respected sire had evidently gone crazy, and that there would be no peace till this interloper was ejected.

In those days as an extra dish, I had octopus to eat and fried sea-slugs. Octopus I like fairly well as an article of diet, but in the long days of collapse that followed these wedding festivities, the food ran very low. I told An senior that I was hungry for meat and that I would be glad to pay a good price for fowl or fish if he could obtain it for me. The next day he came home in great glee, dragging along a huge stinging ray, or skate. "Now we have meat for the stranger," he cried. He washed the loathsome-looking thing at a spring, then divided it and put on salt. For days heaped-up dishes of strong smelling fish spoiled even the rice on my table.

During this time the birds had been company, though we could not capture them for the table. Here where there is really no gunning, various kinds of wild fowl become as tame as domestic birds at home. They stand in groups on one leg eyeing you as you go by. There are several varieties of the egret, the heron, and others more or less interesting. There are paddy birds, who, with their long-billed sisters, stalk about through the mud all day long; so wise they look with their heads to one side, deep in consideration of the respective merits of slug, eel, and tadpole. The tall, stately blue heron, with its pantaloons so tightly keyed up, is one of my most intimate friends of the rice flats of Chosön.

Nearly three months had passed, and I was to leave early next morning for the capital, via the Yellow sea. Notwithstanding the fact that for this time I had heard no English, had seen none of my countrymen, had been living in circumstances so uninviting, there was still an element of sadness in the thought of leaving the place, perhaps never to return. From the mandarin himself down to the coolies I had seen enough to know that there are gentlemen in every nation. They may wear a startling cut of dress; they may believe that the world is flat and that the sun revolves around Korea; they may, in the sultry days of summer, have a weakness for dogflesh—and yet differ much less than we imagine from the average American.

Long since the town with its inhabitants had

grown familiar. Even the dogs seldom gave more than a passing glance or growl, while the little boys would smile at me in proof that our treaty of peace was genuine.

Among those who at the last came to bid me go in peace, were two characters somewhat remarkable. One was the city physician, who though of few words, was looked upon by the people as a man mighty in thought. As for himself, he felt that he was a unit in space, having neither father nor mother, wife nor child. His name was Mr. Moon. I remembered it without difficulty, as the placid brow and far-away expression of the face reminded me of that fair orb. He had a profound way when alone of talking and gesticulating with himself. At such times no doubt his thoughts were deeply professional. Only once did he venture to speak to me of his experience, more particularly in the line of surgery. I asked if he would show me his stock of instruments, that I might compare them with those of the West. At once he took from a cloth wrapper at his side a wooden case. Inside of this, wrapped carefully in paper, were two murderous-looking prongs, such as I had seen boys at home use in eel-fishing. I inquired as to how he used them. There was no reply, but taking one in his hand, he suddenly made a fierce, short gesture, between a guard and a thrust, accompanied by a flash of lightning in his eye; that explained it all. No wonder I had heard frantic cries by night in the direction of Dr. Moon's.

For convulsions he found that a burning ball of moxa punk, or a red-hot cash piece placed on the child's head some two inches above the brow, and left till it had burned sizzling into the bone, served as a never failing remedy. A poultice of cow excrement was good for certain sores. Epidemics he regarded as taxes that were due the great spirits, especially on the part of children, and the more gladly they paid them the sooner the spirit would be pacified. He was a marvel, was Dr. Moon, at acupuncture. He had probed into every joint of the human body, and could run his long needle into unexplored regions two and three inches. "If you do it badly," said he, "the patient dies."

In medicine his great success had rested on the classification of diseases under two heads, desperate cases, and general weakness. For the latter, he prescribed pills made from tiger bones. He reasoned logically that as the tiger is the strongest animal, and the bones the strongest part of him, consequently such pills must be strengthening in any case. For the former, he had a solemn mixture that he spoke of with bated breath. It was made of snakes and toads and centipedes carefully boiled together, and warranted without fail to kill or cure.

For more specific cases he had a list of medicine that ran thus: Musk sack for melancholy, beef's gall for digestion, bear's gall for the liver, dragon teeth for the heart, caterpillars for bronchitis, maggots for delirium, dried snake and cicada skins for cholic.

Such was Dr. Moon as he sat in my room day after day a professional smile playing over his features. I realized that he was no ordinary mortal, but one of the few remarkable men that I had been privileged to know.

The second, a less scientific character, whose good-bye I appreciated even more, was Mr. Quak. My attention was first called to him one afternoon during a disturbance. As I looked out, I saw Quak swinging a heavy club through the air, threatening the life of my best Korean friend. By a little explanation I managed to prevent bloodshed; all quieted down, and ever after Quak and I were friends.

As a coolie he fairly represented his class, and yet there was an air about him peculiarly his own. He talked frequently without taking the pipe from his mouth, or smoked it bowl downward in a free and defiant manner. He combed his hair once a month; and it was said he washed at New Year—as to the latter I have some doubts. His working dress was a pair of wide pantaloons that came to the knees, no coat, no hat, no boots. He did not need these, for though he ate only rice, he was brawny as Tubal Cain. Quak came regularly to our Christian meetings and listened reverently. He thought this religion a very good thing, but as it did not come exactly in the carrying line, it never could be his specialty.

The curse of Korea is that it has so few working men. It is a nation that has wasted away in idleness. It is therefore refreshing to find one whose hands are hard with toil; and such was Quak.

One day a Korean friend and I, upon nearing a mountain pass, saw a coolie coming with an immense load of brushwood on his back. "Surely that is Quak," I said; and Quak it turned out to be, laboring under the hot sun, but able, notwithstanding his burden, to greet us with an Asiatic smile. I said: "Quak, most a mile away I thought it was you." He never forgot the kindness of being thought of by a foreigner for "most a mile."

On leaving that town the morning above mentioned, quite a number of middle and upper class gentlemen, spectacled and dressed in Eastern fashion, came to see me off. Among them, however, was one whose uncombed, sunburned head, contrasted strangely with the others, but whose "go-in-peace" was as genuine as any. He disappeared among the trees; as far as I know, the last of Quak forever.

We had to make some two hundred miles southeastward across this part of the Yellow sea. Our boat was waiting for us, backed up against a sandbar.

An Eastern leave-taking is quite touching. This company of white coats stood on the landing, bowing farewell to the first Westerner who had ever lived for any length of time among them. I really appreciated their kindness, though I fear I expressed it awkwardly. A moment later, I was aboard the junk, up went the sail and we were off to sea.

The craft beneath us was neither barque nor schooner. She carried a prodigious mast that seemed to sweep the sky. I had learned in schoolboy days something about "a good ship tight and free," which I had been in the habit of associating with everything that carried a sail. A little closer examination, however, proved there was no room for poetry about this craft. Her creaking joints and decayed timbers gave evidence that she had entered upon a decline that was likely to be brief. The only thing that at all reassured me, was the old man at the helm, who would have made an excellent representative for the ancient mariner.

Though the boat measured only about eight

feet by twenty, there were in addition to a crew of three, six Korean passengers aboard.

The old sailor had fitted up for my special benefit a stateroom under the after part of the deck. A view of this apartment was obtained by lifting the lid and peering in on hands and knees. The first thing I noticed were two or three rabbits fenced off in one corner, evidently bound for the capital. An, who was still with me, remarked, "We thought you would not object to these T'ok-ki (rabbits). They were imported from China, and we wish to take good care of them." I said, "An, I have no objection to China, but I have to these rabbits; please get them out of this." They were at once shifted forward where they took a steerage passage for the remainder of the journey.

The stateroom was about the size and shape of a coffin, and when the hatches were closed, as dark as the grave itself. The pilot spread his mat and sat just above. My dreams during the voyage were more or less of the nature of suffocation, varying as the old man shifted his position to admit or retard the approach of fresh air through the chinks. Though I lacked oxygen, I was more than supplied with quantities of dust that sifted through, affording ample *material* for breathing.

The breeze that had carried us for some miles seaward, now suddenly died away, leaving us becalmed not far from an island that I had seen indistinctly from the shore. There was no help for it but to pull in and await the tide of the following morning. A Korean sailor must have both wind and tide in his favor before he thinks of moving. With either of these a few points astray, he hauls down the sail and drops anchor. No man, unless he be a marvel of patience, can ever travel successfully by way of the Yellow sea.

The little island that we were approaching looked quite picturesque alone in the water. A mile or so in circumference, it towered to a high cliff at one end; while at the other, it sloped gently down to the sea. A village of seven huts was built on the beach just above high water level. In front of these were the usual groups of white coated natives smoking their pipes and guessing to themselves what kind of cargo this ship would bring. The chief man turned out to be a Mr. Kim, whom I had met not long before on the mainland, and who had made his home out here to carry on fishing. At once I was among friends. They took me to the cliff top where I had a bird's eye view of their island. Round about it was a reef of boulders over which the tide, night and day, tumbled its waters; on its slope were fields of rice and barley; while far beneath were caves that echoed with croaking sea fowl.

SOME OF THE INHABITANTS.

THE HOPE OF THE NATION.

Then I was hurried off to dinner, Kim expressing his regrets the meanwhile that he had nothing better to set before me. The room into which I crawled was, as usual, low and stuffy. I had seen enough of Korean hospitality to expect a sumptuous dinner, notwithstanding Mr. Kim's regrets. And so it was, for a set of tables loaded with everything the sea could provide were placed before me. There were white fish and black fish, fish that looked all tails, eels as boneless and slippery as a Chinaman, double-breasted, armor-plated crabs and lobsters. I ate them without question as to their place in the modern theory of evolution, and found them very palatable. Good-hearted Kim said I had done him honor and put him under deep obligation by eating of his homely fare.

The afternoon was spent exploring caves by torchlight. The natives were delighted by the echo of a revolver shot underground.

As the evening came on I was asked to join a party who were going out to haul in fishing nets. These nets were hung on a wooden framework a few hundred yards from the shore, and were visited twice a day at ebb tide. Eight men propelled the boat by a long oar from the stern. We soon crossed the intervening water, passed under a number of low cables supporting the frame, and then began the haul. The best of those taken belonged to the flounder and turbot species, flat monsters that whipped the salt sea through the air in such a way as to blind us.

As we were returning, I asked the boatmen to sing, to which they responded in true Korean fashion. One would pipe up a peculiar quavering solo, and then would follow a thundering chorus that kept time to the swinging of the oar. Until late at night they sat talking round a fire kindled on the beach. The flames lighting up the dusky group gave another characteristic picture of life in the Hermit Kingdom. Here they lived, cut off from the world, ignorant of everything, full of superstition, and yet having that highest of human virtues—sympathy and love for fellow mortals.

I was recalled to consciousness by the matter-of-fact voice of An, who informed me that he had everything prepared in perfect order to sleep. Quite a large room was awaiting us. I found it by actual measurement to be about fourteen feet long, eight feet wide, and six feet high; but as the accommodation of the village was limited, An asked if he might sleep in the same room and bring a friend or two as well. "Friend, who?" I asked. "Messrs. Choi, Sö, Yi and a few more." My heart sank as I thought of all these natives in that stuffy room. "Bring them in, of course!" A new straw mat was spread out at one end that looked quite inviting. I sat down and waited till these men ranged themselves in a row, while An secured the door and window as though he feared a tiger raid.

Not until I had lain down for a little, did I realize that they had built a tremendous fire in the stoke hole (*agung*), and that the floor was getting hotter and hotter. A little later I shook An up, and we held a consultation. "Why ever did you put on a fire such a warm night as this? I'll roast to death here." An who had been asleep, took a few minutes to realize where he was, and then said the proprietor's wife had done it in spite of his injunctions to the contrary. "But never mind," said An, "I'll fix it all right." He then roused the others, gathered what mats he could, and made me a bed among the rice bags as far distant as possible from the fire, while the Koreans turned themselves over to the heated part, saying it was just the proper temperature for them to sleep comfortably.

Toward morning I awoke partially, with a feeling of suffocation. Though my head seemed to have grown to an enormous size, I was without understanding as to where I was or what was the matter. With a movement that cost an exceeding great effort I sat up, and then the situation dawned upon me. An was out in a flash and had the door and window open. An hour or so later I walked down to the boat, feeling as though I had been exhumed from a burial where all but putrifaction had set in. This was An's greatest failure. I regarded him as the survivors of the Black Hole of Calcutta regarded Suraja Dowlah.

The wind and tide were fair. Soon the junk was flying over the water, carrying us far out to sea, leaving in the distance his island home and the white friendly figure of Mr. Kim.

This was the only day on which we continued to make good time. I was amazed at the youthful way the decrepit junk ploughed along through the water. By five o'clock in the afternoon we had left familiar shore out of sight and were nearing an island called Teung-san. Here we dropped anchor. The island was too large to be measured at a glance. Its thickly wooded hills overlooking the village surpassed in beauty anything I had yet seen in Korea.

Hearing that a *chömsa*, a mandarin of military rank, resided on the island, I took An and went ashore to have an interview if possible. Arriving at the gate quarters, we were stopped by the guard who would neither give entrance nor look at my passport, thinking no doubt that I was a creature from some infernal region. After a little explanation from the all-prevailing

An, we were stationed in the outer guest chamber. In a moment every available space of door and window was taken up by a multitude of peering faces, with as many questions, which An refused to answer until we had seen the mandarin.

One of the guards returned, and announced in tremendous voice that his excellency was ready. To a Western mind the formality of the Oriental is quite overpowering. Poor old Orient! It reminds one somewhat of the tramp, whose training and early opportunities were the best that could be given, but who, through the evils of drink and the misfortunes of his lot, has sunk to rags and destitution; nevertheless the poise of his head and a something in his manner, mark him a gentleman still.

The presence of the official was at first disappointing. He was trembling visibly, and his voice was so unsteady that he could scarcely speak. The reason I cannot tell, unless it be explained by his statement afterward, that no foreigner had ever visited the island before, and that while he had heard of them, he had never seen one. I had the task before me of disabusing his mind, and of leaving a good impression of the foreign world in general. What An thought of it all, I know not, as I never managed to probe so deeply into his soul. The Chömsa proved to be a very genial gentleman, had me stay to dinner with him, and regaled me with stewed cuttlefish and honey water. He walked with us along the wooded pathway back to the boat, remarking how wonderful it was that nations differing so widely in appearance should yet at heart be the same.

Next morning I was awakened by the sound of drums. Had it been one drum, I would have thought nothing of it, but an army of drummers is an oddity in any land; so I climbed on deck to see what it meant. Circling the bay was a line of boats at anchor. Aboard each of these was a Korean sailor beating with two drumsticks as though his life depended on it. Our own boat was no exception, for the round faced boy, whom the ancient mariner called Yöbökki, was taking part in this morning exercise.

Though at a loss to know what this meant, as I had never before witnessed such a sight, I felt interested in the apparent contest that was going on, and charmed at the manner in which Yöbökki did his part. "I'll ask An when he gets up what it means," I thought.

An was what Koreans call a "difficult" man, especially in the morning. The chances were against one's getting any valuable information out of him before ten o'clock; but as my curiosity was aroused I met him when scarcely awake with the question as to what all the drumming meant. "It don't mean anything," said An. "Well now, it is rather peculiar," I remarked, "that Koreans should work so hard, so early in the morning, and all for nothing." Mr. Sö, one of our travelling companions, knowing something of An's peculiar nature, said he would tell me, which he did very nicely. It is a custom among Korean sailors, when signs of rough weather appear to beat drums in prayer, that the god of storms may quiet the sea and send them in safety. It had not occurred to me to think of it in any such connection.

It was indeed a time for men to pray. Scarcely had we been two hours on the open sea that morning, when ragged looking mists came down upon us as though a typhoon were on the way. The wind would whistle as it used to on stormy nights at home. I kept an eye on the old man at the helm, to see if possible in his wintry face some announcement of what was coming; but no signal was given, except an occasional glance at the sail, or a quiet order to Yöbökki. On we scudded; the mists at times lifting would show white caps in all directions. The Koreans, one by one, went below, as they expressed it, "*mopsi apioh*" (miserably sick).

As a choice of two evils I remained on deck, though the salt spray was flying everywhere. Never have I gone so fast, when time, on the other hand, seemed to go so slow. At each plunge the boat echoed as though the waves she rode were armor-plated, while the centre joints at the bending of the mast, gaped ominously. The storm is increasing I know, but what Yöbökki is about I fail to understand. With the help of the other sailor he is bringing rice and fish on deck. What can he mean? Do they intend to dine in the teeth of the raging elements? But no! This is not to be food for mortal man. Gripping the deck to hold themselves in place, they join in repeating a prayer, and then begin pouring rice and fish over the side to propitiate the monster who is hungering for us.

For an hour or so longer we ploughed on expecting each moment to swamp or pitch headlong onto a reef. But suddenly, to my surprise, we found ourselves in calmer water. Not that the wind had gone down, for we still heard the water roaring behind us; but as we saw now through the scattering mists, we were under the lee of an island. I glanced at the old man to see if there was any look of surprise in his face on finding thus unexpectedly a haven of safety, but not a trace of any such expression was there. He looked as though he had struck the exact point that he had been making for for hours. He never saw fine-toothed comb or hair brush, and yet he had proven himself to be a level-headed old man. Eastern storms are violent and of short duration. That evening it quieted down sufficiently to let us make the mainland some miles to the north.

We cast anchor before a desolate looking village. I went ashore with An to have a walk but was followed by such a crowd of sightseers that we had to take refuge in a public house. Here, too, we were almost smothered in the crush.

The leading characters in the place seemed to be a number of clarion voiced females, who, setting all Korean etiquette at defiance, came forth bold as Cæsar to cross-question me. One able-bodied Amazon, smoking a long pipe, pushed to the front, saying, " I'm going to have a look at him—wouldn't they want to see me if I were in his country?" Here I was confronted by one who, like John Knox, feared not the face of man. It was for me to reply in accents humble and low.

At this point An remarked that they were a low rabble and that we had better go aboard.

My heart gave no response of joy at the thought of going back to the junk. Its comforts had grown stale. Our food was rice boiled in a mixture of salt sea water, and fish that had lain on deck till age and sunshine had more than seasoned it. Insects too were waging war upon us.

A night and a day brought no relief. Thirty-six hours later we were still sticking fast in the mud flat where the tide had left us. Time dragged along slowly. I had talked to the Koreans of everything in heaven above and earth beneath that I could get within the limits of my vocabulary; had watched, till I was tired, the slimy things that live in the sea crawling through the mud; had asked how far it was by land to the capital and found it one hundred and fifty miles and no horses to be had.

At last the evening of the fifth day brought relief. Once more we put to sea, the sail full of wind and the old man at the helm. That night we made famous time, for in the morning, eastward, we saw distinctly the hills of Kyöng-keui province. We had entered a peculiar part of the sea, where the rise and fall of the tide is so great that at low water sand flats stretch in all directions with only salt rivers running here and there between.

It was a bright, pleasant day; every man was on deck happy. Even An smiled. We were told, that if the wind kept fair we would make Chemulpo by night. I had faith in the old man, for I had seen that he had had long experience in these waters; one might easily have put it at a hundred years, judging from his clothes or the wrinkles on his brow.

We kept on following the course of one of

these deep sea rivers, until the returning tide lifted us into open water. With the close of the afternoon we sighted the foreign settlement on the hills at Chemulpo, reposing in peace under the beneficent wavings of the Union Jack and the Star Spangled Banner.

My rejoicings at being once more in Western civilization were moderated by the thought of having to leave the ancient mariner and all who had shared my joys and sorrows. On reaching shore, beyond the regular fare, I divided among them the immense sounding sum of one thousand cash, being about twelve and a-half cents for each sailor, and twenty-five for the shaggy old skipper. He seemed deeply moved, as he told me of the pride he had taken in this voyage and that I would be remembered by him for as many years as his hand might hold the rudder.

A little later the boat set sail and the mists closed down upon the water. It was the last of the ancient mariner; and An also with his peculiarities had sailed away.

II

THE COOLIE

Few subjects present more of interest to a foreigner in Korea than the coolie. He it is, who alone exhibits in his person those peculiarities that have been smothered out of his race by fumes of Confucianism. The Koreans having inhaled this teaching from childhood, have gradually lost their natural traits and have become more and more artificial, ever striving to mortify the man that they are, and to put on for new man, a ghost of antiquity. The coolie, however, is not in any such bondage, but exhibits a host of characteristics that make him in some respects the most interesting figure in the land of Morning Calm.

From the first glimpse you have of him you recognize that he is a creature of repose. Nothing should be more restful to a nervous, impatient foreigner, than the sight of a coolie by the wayside, sitting on his heels, or as we generally say, squatting, (sometimes long rows of them), motionless as sea-fowl, indifferent to the heat of the sun, to the flies that congregate upon him, or to the pestiferous gutters that ooze beneath his feet.

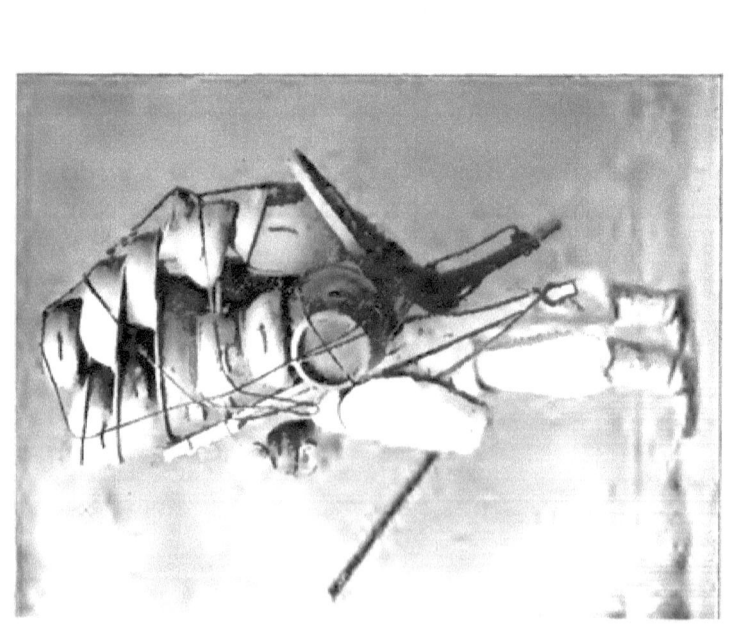

THE COOLIE.

THE COOLIE'S WIFE.

While other mortals are in constant commotion, fearful of this and that, yet aching for change, the Korean coolie continues immovable throughout the ages, the muscles of his heels never growing tired, inhaling all the while atmospheres that would depopulate a Western city, or by way of diversion, eating melons rind and all, in the face of cholera and other Egyptian plagues.

It is an atmosphere of repose rather than indifference, that envelopes him. Indifference suggests an evironment with which one is not in harmony, while repose indicates perfect agreement. Not only can he sit in a painful position for hours, but he can sleep with head down and mouth wide open under the fiercest sun of the Orient, and rise as refreshed as though he had had a night on a spring mattress, followed by a morning bath. This is proof that it is not a matter of indifference with him, else he would have had sunstroke. The fact that he rises refreshed to enjoy his pipe, proves it repose.

Undoubtedly, he is the greatest living example of the absence of all excitement or animated interest of any kind whatever. He can eat an astounding dish of *pap* (rice), and be asleep with his head on a wooden block in less time than a foreigner requires to trim his toothpick. Nothing short of a bowl of vermicelli (*kuk-su*), or the crack of doom, can create the slightest interest in him or prove that he has nerves at all.

This characteristic, while highly to be commended in some respects, has frequently proven a source of difference between the coolie and the foreigner. The latter proud of his watchword—action, runs full tilt into the coolie who sits heavy in repose. It is like a railway train taking a header for a mud embankment—newspapers announce next day, "Smash up"—not of the embankment, but of the railway train.

In view of this danger to the foreigner, the coolie has of late years done considerable to change his ways, although of course, even in foreign employ he still experiences old sensations, and at times falls into his native repose.

Only once do I recollect seeing marked animation in coolies' eyes. It was at a stone fight, such as they used to indulge in in the brave days of old. Several hundred of the best marksmen of the capital chose sides, and armed with stones weighing one and two pounds each, assembled for the fray. When I arrived, missiles were flying through the air, any one of which would have done for a man as easily as a fifty pound projectile. All were alive to the danger, and the rush and scramble to escape was like a stampede of wild beasts. The throwing was magnificent. It seemed, in truth, a little war of giants. The fight grew fast and furious. Begrimed with dust and sweat each side drew in closer, and sent rocks flying through the air in a way that was simply appalling. Then came a shock of cessation, a shout as though a goal were scored; one of the best marksmen of the enemy had been struck squarely, and was killed. His body was carried off the field, and again the fight began. Before evening closed one had fallen on the other side, and thus the score was even.

Such is the coolie, and yet a gentler, more lamb-like creature never lived. Apart from this one ancient custom he is peace itself; even his personal wars are merely threatenings. One of the amusing sights of the street is a fight—the combatants of course always being coolies, as no gentleman would soil his garments who had a servant to engage for him. It usually begins in dispute, passes through different stages, each marked by a special pitch of voice and rapidity of utterance, and at last ends in a climax of fury. A perfect stream of invectives is poured forth, accompanied by appeals to men and angels to behold the object of depravity. A foreigner is horrified, convinced as he is that nothing short of one life can relieve the pent-up condition of affairs; when suddenly the whole case collapses, and the combatants are seen on each end of the piazza, smoking as peacefully as if all within the four seas were brothers.

The question has often arisen, Is the Korean coolie an arrant coward, or is he the bravest man alive since Jack the Giant Killer? Evidence is not lacking for the support of either supposition. On the first announcement of the Japan-China war, we saw him with personal effects on his back and considerable animation in his walk, making for the hills. We have seen him too, in the capacity of trespasser, being whipped out of a compound with a small willow switch, and wilting under the blows as though they had been sword cuts, repeating with imploring look, "Aigo! You've killed me! you've killed me!"

I once had the pleasure of seeing a small foreigner of hasty temperament marshalling his men on a journey. The coolies he had were noted for strength, rather than agility, and as speed was the chief consideration, friction resulted. Matters came to a climax at last, and the small foreigner made a round of those coolies with his right foot, spreading consternation at every kick. No great damage was done, as a Korean's padded dress serves much as a bird's plumage would, under a similar form of attack. The group bowed to the inevitable, simply remarking of the foreigner, that an offspring of his kind was a caution (*Keu nomeui chasik maknanio*).

But there exists just as strong evidence as to the coolie's pluck. He will undergo a surgical operation without flinching where an American would require an anæsthetic. It has been said that he has no nerves, so does not feel it, but he felt the willow switch as keenly as you or I would. Considering his weapons and opportunities, he gave a good account of himself in the old days in the defences at Kang-wha. Often, still, with wretched flint lock or fuse gun, he will steal his way among the rocks, and beard the tiger, capturing his game and returning home in triumph.

Not being able to find a definite example of more than ordinary courage, I referred the matter to my Korean friend, and he told me the following, which in his mind bespoke a heroism rarely seen among mortals: "A number of coolies had imprisoned a huge rat in a grain bin. The question now was, who would venture in bare handed, capture and dispatch the rat. One stout-looking fellow smiled broadly, and amid the applause of the on-lookers, volunteered to go. He pulled his jacket tight, tried his fingers as if to see that all were in working order, and advanced to the attack. Meanwhile the rat facing about, resolved to die game. The parrying lasted a few minutes, then a pass, then a rush of confusion and sudden leap into mid air, all quick as lightning, and the coolie with one hand bleeding, held in the other the lifeless rat. Your common cricket ball," added my Korean friend, "is nothing; but to catch a live rat, which is equal to a cricket ball charged with dynamite, requires courage indeed."

Not only does the coolie at times exhibit surprising agility, but his strength is phenomenal. With a rack made of two forked limbs fastened together, as worn by Mr. Quak, he will carry a bale of piece-goods weighing four hundred pounds, or bring a perfectly paralyzing load of deer hides all the way from Kyüng-heung on the Russian border.

In Korea there are really no carts or wheeled means of transportation. Many of the roads will not admit of beasts of burden, so the strength of the nation has gone into the coolie's shoulders. With a load such as we often see, he reminds one of the Titan Atlas lifting the world.

It has been a sorrow to many a foreigner that the coolie should be so slow in his mental movements, so obstinate about changing his mind or responding to an order, but it is easily explained. Like his body, his mind moves under a pressure of from one to four hundred pounds, which accounts for its slowness of motion. Run violently against his inclinations, and he goes obstinately along, feeling it in fact as little as if you had collided with him when carrying his load of piece goods. Violence wins nothing and means ultimate victory for the coolie. Even in Korea, how many Westerners have spent themselves in a brilliant charge on this coolie phalanx, with apparent victory for the time, but in the end, have won only ignominy, with the name Yang-Kwi-ja (foreign devil) firmly fixed upon them. My dislike for that name is not that it has any deep spiritual signification, but that it is not complimentary and embraces in its scope too many sorts and conditions of men.

This repeated attempt to coerce the Far East, seen, not only in Korea, but elsewhere, has suggested the following lines that are especially applicable to the case of the coolie, though they may possibly have even a wider significance.

> An Occidental newly sent,
>   And keyed up for the tussle,
> Has come to rouse the Orient,
>   And teach it how to hustle.
>
> "This East," he says, "man, woman, child,
>   Is chronically lazy,
> I'll get a move on," and he smiled,
>   "Or drive the country crazy."
>
> He kicked his cook, and sacked his groom,
>   And raised a dire disaster,
> But all in vain his fret and fume,
>   To move the Orient faster.

The horse he rode was like his boy,
  Whose maxim was to-morrow!
His life became instead of joy,
  Accumulated sorrow.

His nerve gave out, his brain went wild,
  Completely off the level,
And, when he died, the Orient smiled,
  "A crazy foreign devil."

In spite of all the pressure, moral and material, that weighs against him, the coolie remains the managing director of the nation, the ornament of every corner and gateway in the city. I reverence him, in fact I always feel respect for any one who has cheated me as successfully and as often as he has. He does it fairly and squarely, a pure matter of business, the sharper man coming out best. On the other hand, sensations of humility creep over me, in remembrance of a saying of my Scotch grandfathers, "wha cheats me aince shame fa' him, wha cheats me twice shame fa' me."

But there is a way to manage the coolie, take him gently and softly at first, with slightly increasing pressure as his being comes into motion, and you can turn him this way and that as by the turning of a rudder; for his condition is not one of obstinacy, but of inability.

It has often been a question, how people who never read employ the mind, and with what do they store it. We can see so little in a lifetime, and can hear so much less at first hand, that we are indebted more largely to literature than to anything else for the delights of life, and for what we know; but the coolie has no literature, yet his mind is stored to repletion; he can entertain you by the hour with tales of impossibilities. To him everything worth repeating must be clothed with the marvellous. Tell him a plain truth, and he will forget it before the morning. Tell him one of the latest yarns, and he will believe it; add to it, and pass it on to the second and third generation. The mind must have its store, and if it cannot obtain it through literature, it will through tradition. Imagine this process going on from father to son for a thousand years, and you can guess the kind of legends and myths that fill the coolie's mind; interesting, some of them are, but quite as far removed from truth as from the generation that began them.

Literature in Korea is a dead letter, so that the interesting field for research is, after all, the beliefs and traditions of the non-reading classes; and the coolie is the only one who possesses these intact. This is by itself so wide a subject that we cannot here touch upon it. His beliefs are legion, though not defined sufficiently to constitute his religion. Articles of dress, trees by the wayside, animals and birds, have endless signs and omens associated with them.

Once while on a journey, my coolie called at my room in the early morning in great distress, saying that the night before he had left his straw shoes to dry in front of the kitchen stoke hole, and that in the dark before the dawn they had been swept into the fire and burned. As they cost only a few *cash*, we tried to comfort him by saying he could have another pair, but he said, "No! no! that's not it. To burn your shoes is an omen. I shall die." I tried to reason him out of it, but he was fixed in his faith, and that day went with doleful face till we reached the capital. Two days later he sent saying he was very ill. I had a foreign physician see him, who pronounced his case typhus. The poor coolie with a most lugubrious face reminded me of the omen three nights before, as much as to say, that he and his straw shoes knew more in half an hour than I could tell them in years.

Independence is a new thought to Korea, and a new word has been coined to express it. The native has never dreamed of an existence apart from that of others. In the Western world, a man may bear his own burden, just as a house may stand by itself in a wide expanse of country; but in the Orient men work in groups, and houses draw together into hamlets and villages. The great forces with us are centrifugal, marked by extension, separation, and the like; while in the East, life tends toward the centre, and is characterized by contraction and limitation, the coolie being one of the largest factors in this process. The sphere of his usefulness is so contracted in fact, that he will undertake nothing without an assistant. He eyes the simplest task with a look of despair, unless you will engage his friend as well. Should it be the handling of a wood-saw, he must have a coolie at the other end; not from necessity, but because it is custom and conforms to the eternal fitness of things.

His use of a shovel too is striking. A description of this I will quote from my friend the Rev. G. Heber Jones, one of the closest observers and best students in Korea. "This interesting invention occupies a front rank among labor-saving machines of Korea, for it saves from three to five men a vast deal of work. It consists of a long wooden shovel, armed with an iron shoe, to cut into the earth properly. The handle is about five feet long, and is worked (to a certain extent) by the captain of the crew. Two ropes, one on each side, are attached to the bowl of the shovel, and these are managed by the men who seek to save their labor.

"While in operation the captain inserts the iron-shod point of the shovel sometimes as deep into the earth as three inches, and then the crew of two or four men give a lusty pull and a shout, and away will go a tablespoonful of earth fully six feet or more, into the distance. This operation is repeated three or four times, and then the weary crew take a recess, and refresh themselves with a pipe. It is a beautiful sight to watch a crew working these power shovels; everything is executed with such clock-like regularity, especially the recess. They sometimes sing in a minor strain—for the Korean coolie can always be depended on, when putting in his time, to do it in as pleasant a manner as possible.

"That this implement belongs to the class of labor-saving machines there can be no doubt. It takes five men to do one man's work, but entails no reduction in the pay. In fact, the number of the crew can be extended to the limit of the shovel's ropes without risk of a strike among the laborers. Many interesting stories might be told to illustrate its name of the power shovel, one of which I will tell: We had a small patch of ground we wanted turned over, so we hired a coolie, and put into his hand a beautiful new spade from America. He attached two straw ropes to it, hired four other coolies, at our expense of course, and did the job in triumph. Such is the power of this instrument over the Korean coolie's mind."

No amount of money can tempt the coolie to

break faith with custom. He regards money as a convenience, but in no case as a necessity. Other things being satisfactory he will agree to accept of it, will demand more at times, or will regard with a look of scorn the largest amount you can offer him. He never descends to purely business relations. When you engage him for a piece of work he comes simply with a desire for your convenience, while in the evening you present him with cash expressive of your friendship and appreciation. Should the relations during the day become strained, he will probably demand more; should friendship be strengthened, he will accept less; should mutual disagreement break out, he will not work for you for any money, and in all probability will have you boycotted by others of the village.

The coolie's religion consists in a worship of ancestors, and a hatred of all officialdom; not that he really loves the former, or dislikes the latter; but custom requires that he attribute success to the virtue of his forefathers, and failure to the depravity of the district mandarin; hence expressions of reverence for the one, and sworn hatred for the other.

In the first prefecture I visited, the coolies of the village spent a large part of their time squatting on their heels, anathematizing the prefect who lived over the hills in the *yamen*. It seemed to me we were on the eve of an uprising that would leave not even cotton wadding enough to tell of the fate of the hapless magistrate. During the course of the season, we became acquainted, and a more sleek, contented official it has never been my fortune to know—wholly oblivious he seemed to the storm brewing about his ears. The storm continued to brew, but never broke. Visits to other parts of the country have since demonstrated beyond doubt, that this discontent is the normal condition of affairs in Korea; and that the prefect would never be happy or safe without this centripetal force to keep him within a reasonable orbit.

While cherishing such hatred on the one hand, the coolie is quite emphatic in his loyalty to the king on the other. To him, his majesty is the peerless perfection of wisdom and benevolence—one who in fact cannot sin; who though as wicked as Nero and unscrupulous as Ahab, would be spoken of as the son of divinity, the sinless jăde ruler, etc.; while the officers who surround him from ministers down, are regarded as public outlaws, veritable banditti of state.

The coolie has no visible fear of his fellow man. His enemies are *tokgabi* and *kwisin*, which might be translated "little devils." He regards all distasteful conditions of life as under their control, and the earnestness with which he sets himself about the capture of the "little devil," and the corking of him in a bottle, and the burying him deep underground, has marked many an anxious line across the coolie's face, that was never marked by ordinary care or fear of mortal man. It takes the larger part of his personal earnings to pay *P'ansu* (blind fortune-tellers) and *Mutang* (sorceress) who come and dance and shout with cymbals and drums and gongs—enough to scare any devil. I have watched a sorceress when exorcising some spirit. She seemed in a state of ecstatic exhilaration, whirling and turning, until my own sight most lost its balance, and I saw no reason why I should not step into the circle and waltz round to.

The poor coolie lives in constant dread lest even his topknot be not safe. A passing devil may cut it off in the dark, so he seldom goes out at night. Some who have had their topknots thus stolen have come and told me. Devils set fire to the house by throwing a ball of living flame against the thatch. This ball the *tokgabi* have brought all the way from Pluto's furnace. Dishes go clash, bang, in the kitchen without visible cause, while water is heard being dashed against the wall. Meanwhile, the door is drawn tighter, the lock doubly fastened, and the wife trembling exclaims, these devils are worse than any mother-in-law.

I have often wondered where all the wrinkles come from on the face of the coolie, when he takes life so evenly and is so indifferent about work. I conclude that they come from fear of devils, who through the coolie's lifetime hold him in bondage.

The coolie's relation to his deceased ancestors I have never been able to define. That he is devout in the performance of the sacred rites, is unquestioned; but that he has a clear understanding of their purport, is exceedingly doubtful. A proof however of his grasp of the situation is seen in this, that he can point you out every grave of his ancestors to the fourth generation, and can talk as familiarly of a great-grandfather's second cousin as we could of a half sister. No spirit is forgotten in his round of yearly sacrifice. As to what it all means he leaves you in doubt. Prosperity in some mysterious way hangs upon it, and there the subject rests.

I have often thought—though my Korean friend says it is not so—that the native carries a grudge against his deceased parent, such as an accomplice might feel toward one who had turned state's evidence. The parent departs this life, and in so doing, commits a heinous breach of propriety, leaving his posterity to bear the disgrace, while he is picnicking with his seniors and other distinguished spirits of antiquity. Calling himself "depraved existence," "unconscionable sinner," the coolie mourner wanders for three years with a burden on his heart, and the shade of a wide hat over his countenance.

The coolie's home life is simple. A mat or two on the mud floor, with a fire underneath, is comfort enough for the most fastidious. His iron jointed, supple sinewed wife, keeps all in motion. The Korean would long since have been reduced to dust and ashes had it not been for her. While her husband sits and smokes, she swings her batons, making the kitchen ring with her voice or the sounds of the cooking. Though unacquainted with the embroidered side of life, she is a faithful, decent woman, and does honor to the Far East. True to her husband, and kind to her children, in spite of her unattractive appearance and emphatic manner, she takes her part in the struggle of life bravely and modestly, and does credit to womankind the world over.

But now as we leave the coolie let us remember only his virtues. He takes life as it comes, and is always good-natured. Be it rough or smooth he shines with content. He seldom washes, has no second change of clothing, no carpets or slippers. He eats any kind of food, sleeps on the roadway when night overtakes him, and lies down to die with as little ceremony as he lives. A rough, craggy kind of life, where strength of body and mind might both develop. Korean philosophy says strength, not beauty, is what men need. "Strength is the male, beauty is the female": and the coolie is strong.

You are never through with him, nor is he ever through with you. He jostles you on the streets, wipes his oily shoulders on you as he goes by, bows and smiles as sweetly as though his life were a holiday and his conscience clear.

One coolie stands out prominently before me, a little man with brown face who accompanied me on trips into the interior, keeping the way clear, and acting throughout in my interest. One evening after a bleak day of nearly forty miles of travel, we entered quarters for the night, and were informed that there was no room, nothing to eat, and no use for a foreigner. All the town apparently had come out to tell us so. Here I was alone in the world, no one to depend on but the little man with brown face, and he had run forty miles already. Not wearied, but simply shortened in temper, he spent about eight seconds arguing the question with the towns-people, and when that did not avail, turned on the chief speaker, a tall lanky fellow, and taking a double hold of the after-part of his garments ran him down that street as though propelled by a locomotive. This was conclusive proof to the inhabitants that we, not they, were running the town, so they yielded us a room, rice and eggs, and comfort for the night.

Many a day since, all my hopes have been centred in the little man with brown face, and never once has he failed me; but has carried me on his back over streams, stood by through rain and snow—ever forgetful of his own comforts; has been the life of the party, providing situations of amusement clear across the peninsula; trustworthy as one's brother, and faithful as the sun—all for what? A few cash that he could have earned with much less labor upon his own mud floor at home; but down in his coolie's heart, it was for him a matter of friendship and honor.

It is long now since a difference of location compelled us to separate, but frequently still, by post or courier, comes a thick wadded letter written in native script, wishing long life and blessing; saying that he still lives and is well; signed awkwardly and humbly by the little man with brown face.

III

THE YALU AND BEYOND

In giving a faithful account of a journey in an Eastern country there are many things to be mentioned that are other than pleasing. One endeavors, as far as possible, to see with a halo round each eye; but in spite of such effort, the shock is often great for a tender, Western nervous system, so that it were best not to peer too closely into the mysteries of Oriental travel.

Koyang is a little town of no importance, twelve miles northeast of Seoul. Here our party arrived about dark, and dined on rice, red peppers, and fish spawn, under the inspiration of which repast we turned in for the night.

We had started from Seoul about noon, with two ponies so piled up with bundles that scarce anything could be seen of the original animals. In our party was a Mr. Sö, a Korean of considerable culture, who had spent most of his life in China and on the border land. We invited him to accompany us, first, because he was a pleasant gentleman, and second, because he spoke Chinese, and we did not know but we might go through Manchuria before returning. He was the awe-inspiring member of the party and lent it dignity. His monstrously padded clothes and huge black spectacles gave him the appearance of a double-eyed cyclop. His long pipe however reassured one, and demonstrated to the world that he was not a creature to be feared, but a gentle being of refinement and culture.

We took along a boy called Keumdoli, a good-natured youth, whose face had been pimpled into a kind of pebbled leather by the smallpox.

Another member of the party was a half-grown terrier, who cut capers as though he were going on a picnic of an hour or two, instead of a journey of a thousand miles. He dived about here and there, and looked so nimble, that the natives were inclined to view him, not as a *canis*, but as a *kwisin* (spirit) which these Westerners had taken along for congenial company. We called him Nip. He was the genteel Western member of the party.

Koyang was peaceful and quiet after Seoul. We slept well, and next morning entered through a narrow pass into what is known as the robber district. We saw no highwayman, and the ordinary passers looked at our dog and not at us.

Apart entirely from brigands, there are historical reminiscences connected with this place. Five centuries ago, when Song-do was capital, this mountain district was filled with some hundred and more Buddhist temples. During that dynasty, which was favorable to Buddha, they remained unmolested, but upon the establishment of royalty in Hān Yang (Seoul), the Buddhists were routed out, and their temples burned. "Only one trace of them remains to-day," said Mr. Sö, "in springtime, the stones are lined with a yellow coating of bedbugs that have faded somewhat for having remained five hundred years without the proper means of subsistence." I am informed, in all seriousness, that notwithstanding their long fasting some still weigh as much as half a pound.

A little further along we came on two *miryök* or colossal Buddhas, looking down from the mountain side with the everlasting apathy of Sukamoni written on their faces. It is the Sphinx and his wife, the riddle of the Far East standing out before you. They were chiselled from the solid rock, six or seven centuries ago, when Song-do was the capital. Song-do had looked with anxiety upon the increasing influence of Hān Yang. Its soothsayers likened the mountains around Seoul to a huge cat, ready to pounce upon the rat hills of Song-do. The King of Koryö, in fear lest he might perish along with the rats, caused his people to cut these *miryök* so as to face Seoul and guard Song-do.

On the afternoon of February 29th, after a tiresome walk, we came suddenly through a hill pass overlooking the Im-chin river. The ice in breaking up, had formed a jam just in front of the gate which blocked our way, and nothing remained but to slide horses, men, and baggage over a neighboring slope and catch a boat further up where there was open water. The interesting feature of our descent, was the horseman's bringing the two ponies. He took a firm hold of the halter of one, tugged him into motion, made a bound for the edge, and never looked back until he had reached the bottom. The pony slid, and rolled, and in a twinkle was at the foot too, apparently very much to its own surprise; the other followed in like manner. Three or four towsy-headed natives propelled us over in a scow that leaked ominously. At last they landed us, partly by carrying us on their backs, and partly by dumping us into the water, and, withal, amid great noise and confusion. Ten *li* further on we found an inn, where they kindled a fire beneath the floor, that not only warmed, but baked us the livelong night. This is only a trifling matter, and yet it is not as easy to endure the baking process gracefully, as a cold outsider might imagine.

On a promontory overlooking this river, which is called Im-chin, we noticed a monumental building, quite insignificant in appearance, and yet there is associated with it an oft-repeated Korean tale:—About four centuries ago there lived a prophet, called Yül-gok, who built here an oddly shaped structure. It was his custom frequently to oil the woodwork, inside and out, and, when asked the meaning, said he was preparing it to be burned. Said he, punning on the name of the river, "among the years to come, in the one called Im-chin, on a certain night (giving the date) this building must be fired, or great disaster will overtake the nation." Before the year of his prophecy had come, Yül-gok fell sick and died, leaving his older brother to keep the house oiled, and burn it on the appointed night. With the year Im-chin (1592), came the invasion of the Japanese, and their march on Seoul. The Korean king fled for his life. In the night, almost alone, he was trying in vain to find his way over these mountains, expecting every moment to be captured by those following hard after him. When darkness seemed to render escape impossible, suddenly a fire blazed up from a point just ahead, lighting the surrounding country. By means of it the king made his way over the mountains, across the river, and ultimately escaped. This was the predicted night and the oiled house of the prophet had saved the king. Now, upon the same promontory stands the building we had seen, in modest commemoration of the prophet's wisdom.

The weather this day had been balmy and springlike—some of the willows already showed signs of life. On these and other trees by the roadside rags were tied, while underneath stones were heaped up. This is one Korean method of charming away the ill-luck that devils are supposed to be constantly inflicting upon mortals. There is no special sacred tree in Korea, as this day we passed an oak, a maple and a cedar, all of them hanging with spirit offerings. According to Korean demonology, a tree is supposed to be the abiding place of various kinds of evil spirits. Inside of the bark and roots, everywhere in fact, legions of these are secreted. My boy awoke me one night, saying that he could not sleep, because devils were throwing sand against the window, and that they were coming out of an old tree behind the house. I went out to investigate, and found chips scattered about giving forth a pale phosphorescent light that the boy was sure were devils.

The next day we were to enter Song-do the capital of the Wangs, the kings of the former dynasty. Rain came on and drowned our enthusiasm and made walking anything but pleasant. One of the signs that we were approaching the city was the hats we saw. They are of a shape peculiar to this district; are made of straw, wide, pointed, and umbrella-like. They resemble the hats worn by the Buddhists, and have come down from a time when it was fashionable to dress as Buddha did. About three o'clock we passed through a long, tablet-lined street, and put up at an inn just outside the South Gate. Here we waited till seven P. M. for lunch. One grows to be patient and long-suffering in Korea, and, certainly, the sooner he becomes so the better for him. The only way to be happy, when travelling, is to give Koreans time. Let them work out their part of the pilgrimage in their own way. It is altogether useless to labor, and fret, and hurry them, for they will be just as slow as ever, and love you the less withal. Rather strange it is that a land so tedious should be so rich in the "hurry up" style of word. *Ossa, quippe, ullin, söki, balli, patpi, chiksi, chankam, souipki, nalli nankum* are a few of the more common that we try and that we hear every day. The native hears them too, and they have as much effect on him as paper balls would have on ten inch armor-plate.

We remained a few days in Song-do, meditating over its ruins. In the terraced ground the foundations are still solid, and cut stones are tumbled here and there reminding us of the ancient palace that fell when the Angevins were ruling in England. The city contains some 50,000 inhabitants and lies at the foot of the Song Ak mountain. It has a sad, antiquated look. Only a few buildings remain inside the walls, and these are well on the way to ruin.

Hereabouts we found a number of ginseng fields. Sheds, some three and a half feet high and of about the same width, are arranged in rows, the earth is built up under these, and neatly kept in place by slates; and here the ginseng grows.

Ginseng is Korea's elixir of life, the one great cure-all for mortal ailments. The cultivated variety is valuable—very valuable in fact; but the value of the mountain variety no one knows. Men search for it as they seek gold in the Klondyke. The mania grows on them; many seekers are driven mad and disappear in the mountains. We are told too that mortal vision is not sufficient for the search; that ginseng flowers are only seen by the spiritually enlightened—for the gods alone have to do with them.

Every official carries among his choicest treasures a few roots of ginseng. Like whiskey in Scotland, it will warm you when cold and cool you when heated. It makes the aged young and spry, and gives the fading mother a new lease of life.

H. H. Yi Chun Yong, whom I had the honor of meeting frequently in Japan, enclosed to my address once, along with some valuable relics of Korean art, a bundle of ginseng marked "eat and live." I ate of it—and still live.

We also visited a far-famed quarter by the east wall. There is a stream here, with a stone bridge that has been partly railed round. Why the railing? Because of one sacred stone in the middle, on which are marks like blood. The story goes that at the fall of Song-do a certain Prince Cheung, who refused homage to the usurpers, while riding back to the city was murdered on this bridge. His blood sank into the stones, and five hundred years cannot wash out the stains. The natives believe implicitly in the legend, and to the present reigning family this bridge has ever been a sort of Banquo's ghost.

Leaving the old capital, our road led northward through a mountainous district, cut here and there with slate quarries. On the first day out, being tired from the heavy roads, we stopped at an inn where a woman seemed to be the sole manager. We felt sorry for her at first, for she looked as though all the seats of war since the Song-do dynasty had been mapped upon her face; but on further acquaintance we grew to fear her—there was a keen edge to her voice that made us reply in accents meek and low. Her toilet was grimy with time and smoke and was so arranged that everything seemed to centre just under her arms giving her a warlike as well as a domestic air. She smiled, and said kind things about our dog, so that we felt considerably drawn to her. Indeed we mention her because she is one of the few characters whom we still see in memory.

At the highest point of the road was a shrine to some spirit or god supposed to be in possession of the place. Inside of it was the common picture we see of a Korean riding upon a tiger. We noticed that the natives spoke respectfully of the tiger, calling him San-yüng-gam (the old gentleman of the mountain). They have all learned in Korea to be polite to their superiors —which accounts for this and the offerings that were made before the shrine. We felt, however, that a more likely party to fear was the old lady at the foot of the hill; and in case of any deviltry in those parts, we should make our offering to her, and give the tiger and *kwisin* (the demon) a second place.

After a journey in all of some two hundred miles, we sighted the historic city of P'yöng-yang. It stands on the right bank of the Tatong river, which here flows south. The approach through an avenue of trees skirting the bank is full of picturesqueness. The crossing made, we entered the East Gate into perhaps the busiest city in Korea. Not its business however, but its antiquity is of special interest. To Koreans it is all sacred ground, for this was Keui-ja's home something about the time King David reigned in Jerusalem, and Keui-ja is the father of Chosön.

Koreans speak of P'yöng-yang as the boat-shaped capital. The walls were outlined on this plan by its first founder, and it is still the floating city. No one is supposed to dig for water anywhere inside the walls, as that would be cutting through the bottom and sinking the ship. For this reason water is carried from the river even to the most distant quarters, and the peculiar gait of the water-carrier is one of the oddities of the street. The streets we found to be, as usual, narrow and filthy and crowded with shops of native wares. The people, whom we had often heard to be more warlike and independent than other hermits, seemed to us in their appearance and disposition a very ordinary lot, perhaps a little less noisy and somewhat more polite than the natives of the south. Among the hills to the north are the Buddhists. Here they have a citadel of temples commanding an excellent view of the river. Its beauty and strength of situation gives one an idea of the power Buddha once possessed in Chosön.

To the south, offsetting this, is the Woi söng (outer city), where the ancient palace of Keui-ja stood, and where his descendants still live. These ancients look upon present rank as but a ghost of nobility. Like the Jews, they feel that they are still the chosen people. So they and the Buddhists live, shut off from the city by massive walls, and from the world by centuries of time. One would think that they might enjoy each other's company, for we can scarcely imagine companions more likely to be congenial than an aged priest and an old soldier.

Since this journey, the city of P'yöng-yang has experienced the misfortunes of war. For a time it was the centre of interest. The Chinese marched in with the display and confidence that ignorance gives, and there wasted their time and strength in meaningless delay. The Japanese meanwhile, took possession of every means of exit and approach, and when their numbers had increased to the point where victory was insured, they fell upon their foes as wolves would upon sheep. The Chinese in hopeless confusion, fifty thousand of them at once, trampled each other in a wild rush for the North Gateway, intending to take the shortest and surest route for China. But some one had lost the key and there was no egress. Back they came for the South Gate like so many beasts in stampede, only to be mowed down in all directions. It was not a battle, but a slaughter of helpless creatures who had not intelligence enough to plan an escape, much less a campaign in modern warfare. The society for the prevention of cruelty to animals should extend its beneficent influence to the Far East, and put a ban on shooting inoffensive Chinamen, soldier or civilian.

After the slaughter, the city of P'yöng-yang was strewn with corpses, and the once busy streets were silent, for the inhabitants had scattered, no one knew whither. A Korean with his wife and three children, escaped through the thick of the fight, and by climbing the wall reached safety. He had been a man of some means, but of course had lost everything. He said he was thankful he had his three children spared to him. The little black-eyed girl had heard and seen that night what she would never forget—the rattle of Murata rifles and the other hideous accompaniments of war.

Many droll stories are told of the Oriental's ideas of warfare. Chinese cavalrymen came riding to the charge with fans and perfume bottles, while a servant brought up the rear with a Winchester rifle.

Most of those who later on came to the dispensary in Mukden for treatment were wounded in the back. "How is it that sons of the gods are wounded in their afterparts only?" asked the foreigner. "It looks as though they had run from the barbarians." "We advanced all right," says the Chinaman; "according to military methods. Then we put on fierce faces like *Che-kal-yang*, the God of War, certain that the *Wo-jen* would run, as they should have, were they not hopeless savages, and unacquainted with Chinese characters. We rushed on them breathing forth fire, but they moved not. Then our general shouted Victory! for we had paralyzed them with our boldness. But suddenly a long row of guns raised like one arm, and, immortal gods! such a dastardly way to fight I never saw! I know not why we were wounded in the back."

For the few days that we remained in P'yöngyang, we were followed by an innumerable company of spectators, whose outbursts of laughter, as we walked along, seemed to betoken something extraordinary in our personal appearance. Nevertheless we walked the streets until we made our final exit in safety, through this Chinaman's trap, the North Gateway. Snow had fallen, and the roads were muddy and unpleasant. A few days more carried us out of the flat valleys, past Anju, and Pak-chön, to where the road was lifted high and dry, affording glimpses of the Yellow sea to the left.

We spent a pleasant day in a town called

Kasan, and when we left, a few of the natives saw us safely out of the village and then threw stones after us. Fortunately they did not throw with the same precision that they do in Whang-hă, so we remain to tell our story.

A little later, we passed a mound of some interest, called the Speaking Grave, which came by its name in an extraordinary way. About a hundred years or so ago, there came by a traveller, who, through unexpected delay, was overtaken by night. He saw before him the craggy pass over which we had just come, and fearing that tigers might be prowling about, made up his mind to sleep till daylight beside a grave that he found among the trees. About midnight, he was awakened by a voice across the valley. "Hollo! Isn't to-morrow the anniversary of your burial!" Before there was time to imagine what such a question could mean, he heard a reply come from the grave beside him, "Yes of my burial!" "In that case," said the other, "you'll go and see that the sacrificial food is ready in your home, will you not?" "I would go," said the voice in reply, "but I have a guest sleeping here and cannot leave." "Aha!" said he across the valley, "I see, but then if you go, I'll be host till you return." "Thanks!" said the ghost, and all was silent. He went, but soon returned announcing his presence by sounds of fury. "Here already!

how so soon?" asked the host pro tem. "Fiends!" said he, "what a mess!" which was the only reply, till, cooling off a little, he added, "I went to the house, saw the food, and right in the middle of it, what think you? a snake coiled about. I have just sent a posse of hobgoblins for my youngest grandson. I'll teach them to offer me snakes!" The ghosts expressed mutual horror, and all was silent. When morning came, our traveller hurried to a village near by, and inquired about the man buried yonder, who he was, and where he had lived. Arriving at the home, he found it was indeed the anniversary of the old man's funeral. Breathlessly he asked if all were well. Alas! no, their little boy had been drowned that night. He then explained what he had heard in the valley, and what the cause of it had been. "A serpent in the sacrificial food, where?" they asked "where?" Searching carefully each dish, they found nothing that could resemble this except a long hair, which they at last concluded the ghost, with his transcendental vision, had taken for a serpent. The Speaking Grave is now carefully guarded and is one of the sacred groves on the way north.

In the town of Yong-chön, our attention was called to a peculiar custom that I have seen nowhere else in Korea. We had stopped at an inn filthy beyond all description, and after getting seated on as clean a spot as possible, we noticed what might be called a dagger in the ridge-log above us. It seems to have been a custom handed down from their ancestors. Should one die in the village on an unlucky day, they say the soul travels about, entering other homes with intent to carry off the living. On entering, he glances at the ridge-log; a dagger sticking there will scare him off and save the inmates.

We felt how invulnerable we were before these imaginary evils, when suddenly we were attacked by enemies that outrival all superstition. It was the old story of roaches and bugs. Koreans say that roaches eat bugs, and again I have been told that bugs turn into roaches when they get old. Of one thing only am I certain, that both roaches and bugs eat mortal man, and neither one nor the other ever seems to grow old or to transmigrate into anything less objectionable.

On an afternoon in March, as we were journeying along in an indifferent way, Sö suddenly called our attention to a range of peaks dimly outlined before us. "That," said he, "is China beyond the Yalu." It was the first that we had seen of the Celestial Empire, and our hearts awoke as we recalled what we had heard of that far-famed land. Suiting a familiar metaphor to our surroundings, we felt that long centuries, almond-eyed and cued, were looking down upon us from the height of yonder mountains.

On we journeyed, gradually ascending until we entered Eui-ju, a modest town pleasantly situated looking south over the Yalu. It is a quaint, old-fashioned place, and might be called an Asiatic Antwerp. There were Chinese merchants, and a few Koreans engaged in business, but all spoke of trade as being dead now in contrast to some period before the opening of the treaty ports. Eui-ju, like the rest of Korea, is in poverty and ready to die of starvation. The products of the soil and manufactures are gradually growing less, while the mints are rolling out inferior copper cash. On a small scale it reminds one of France in 1774. It is the old question of differences of rank that threaten the existence of the nation; in other words, is it better to be an immaculate, laundried aristocrat (*yang-ban*), and die of starvation in a dignified manner, or to become a low class man and work out one's salvation with sun-tanned face and hardened hands?

The nakedness of the land too makes one sad, "*C'est triste*," said a French father to me when looking at its brown hills. There is really no timber in Korea. There are indeed a few scattered remnants of what were doubtless forests in former times, but there remain no heavily timbered lands.

On an April morning we crossed the river flats and the three divisions of the Yalu. Our dog cut capers on the sand banks, joyful no doubt in the thought of exchanging half-famished Korea for great, porky, greasy, oily China.

Only the Yalu divides these two, and yet they differ vastly. Dress, occupation, food, language, everything was new to us. Korea, idle or asleep; China, strange to say, awake and busy! Having asked for an inn, we were shown into a place that was blue with smoke. We resolved to wait outside until it had cleared away a little, but Păk, a friend whom we met at Eui-ju, told us it was always so in a Chinese inn, and that we must get used to it. So in we plunged. Chicken coop, pigpen, kitchen, sleeping apartments, were all one and the same room. Under greasy blankets lay Chinamen—some asleep, some puffing away at opium, others again half-dressed searching the seams of their clothing in a suspicious way, all more or less attracted by our arrival: for Western people are rare here.

Razor-backed pigs walked about the ground floor, indifferent to the fate of their relatives in the frying-pans just above them. The host brushed back and forth, keeping the on-lookers at a distance, as though he felt much responsibility on our behalf. Groups of oily urchins gathered about us. One little fellow, after looking at me for a moment, shouted "Yang

Kwe ja!" and ran, the proprietor following him in a most threatening manner. We felt that this "Kwe ja" must be an interesting word, and so looked it up in the lexicon, where it read "devil's son" or "foreign devil."

The dinner which they brought in consisted of strings of pork, vermicelli, and scrambled eggs. We looked at the pork, and then at the live pigs grunting by us, and considered how narrow the step between them and death. The eggs, of which there might have been a dozen on each plate, were so excessively scrambled that my companion declared a sight of them was enough for him. The vermicelli passed on its way with such rapidity of motion that there was really no time to taste it. We all dined squeamishly, except the dog, who fairly revelled in oil, and so continued from this day till we recrossed the Yalu a month later, three hundred miles further up.

Our carts were already in waiting, three mules on each, one in the shafts, one to the right, and one ahead. The one in the shafts was so time worn that his hide was bare in patches; nevertheless he settled himself down to work in a way that showed he was still master of the situation. These carts are strongly built, and as we found afterward, can bump their way over all manner of rocky roads without being any the worse for it. To increase comfort, and also to cheer our hearts on the way, Keumdoli had cushioned us carefully with bundles of Chinese confectionery.

Our passports were asked for and sent into the *yamen*, and then six soldiers and a mounted officer came to pilot the way. Though not a fighting soldiery, they served admirably as a picturesque guard of honor. They assured us that we were safe in their hands from Manchurian brigandage. The chief gave us his name, and said he was a Mohammedan. On further inquiry, it would appear that Manchu Moslems have little or no knowledge of the Koran, their principal tenet being sworn enmity to pork, in which respect I should be a Mohammedan too, if I lived in Manchuria.

The first afternoon gave us some idea of the great difference between Korea and China. The people were all busy, either with carts, or carrying loads, or out working every foot of arable land; no loungers anywhere. Even the Koreans across the line seemed to have breathed a new life, and were at work something like men. One uncombed hermit remarked that he did not mind the work, but the food was so unclean that no mortal man could eat it.

The next day at noon we entered the town of Whong-hong-san. On the way in we met several detachments of cavalry, dressed in flashing colors. They looked little like Western troops, but were quite as picturesque, and rode splendidly, none of that hang-on-with-both-hands that we see so much of in Korea. In the inn where we lunched, soldiers were quartered. These were armed with English "Tower" rifles that were out of date in Europe long ago, but are still quite abreast of the times in Manchuria. While expecting the contrary, we found the natives much quieter and more orderly than in Korea.

We pushed on making thirty-five miles a day. The wretched carts had been carefully padded before starting, but no padding will ever suffice. They were bumped, and tossed, and tumbled. Less than two days taught us just to hold on in mortal terror. Although winding along the valley, our way had been a gradual ascent until the evening of the second day. After losing the road once or twice in the darkness, the muleteers lit their lanterns and we entered a cutting wide enough for one cart only. This continued for a mile and more, until we had passed into the depths on the other side of the ridge. Had we met carts here I have never yet solved the question as to how we would have passed. Nothing came to stop our progress, and at last, we reached the summit where we rested for a little. The China boys adjusted the harness, examined the carts closely, and trimmed their lanterns afresh. Then began the descent. From the first it was steep, but gradually grew steeper. The old mule who was responsible for our lives, as well as for the confectionery on board, did his part amazingly well. Even when the shafts seemed to point nearer and nearer toward the centre of the earth, never a false step or unguarded movement. Round we went in the glimmering light, down deeper, deeper. "John" labored along by the side, holding to the shafts. He had a mysterious way of regulating the speed by a chucking in his throat, which the patchwork mule seemed to listen for with long and attentive ears. Next morning, when we emerged from the inn at the foot and looked back on the mountains down which we had come so skillfully, we could not but feel a deep admiration in our soul for that old pilot-mule.

In the upper mountain regions it snowed, and lower down it rained. For five days we labored through a terribly mountainous district. Though not the best time of year to judge we could see that the valleys were exceedingly fertile and that every piece of land was carefully cultivated. On the mountain sides were goats and sheep grazing, and sometimes a few cattle. We saw but little timber on this part of our journey. It was upon our return eastward that we came upon forest lands.

On the afternoon of the fifth day we emerged from the mountains into what seemed like northwest prairie lands. Already we were within sight of the city of Nay-yang, the largest on the way to Mukden. It seemed composed of pagodas, grotesque roofs, and gateways. We approached the east gate, but without going in, merely skirting the walls and turning northwest through the flat lands. The country here is beautifully cultivated and dotted with villages. Domestic life, though filthy, has a prosperous appearance. Chinese gentlemen speak of Manchuria as the foul quarter of the empire. The worst feature of the country is the roads. Highways in China being left to care for themselves have fallen into a most unhappy condition. We foolishly imagined, before reaching the plain, that we would have a rest, and find it smooth after the mountains, but the last thirty-five miles were the worst of all. Chinese carts, too, are the cruelest vehicles that a mortal ever boarded. Added to other inconveniences the wind for the last day was in our faces, keen as a knife, blistering wherever it touched. It must have come straight from the steppes of Siberia or some other frozen region. So unbearable was it, that we had to hide our faces, and so miss much of the view of the approach to Mukden. Sand was also flying hideously. That afternoon the mules dragged us into our destination and deposited us in an inn-yard just outside the city wall.

I shall not attempt a description of the place. We visited the Temple of the Fox, Mohammedan Mosques, etc., and saw what interested us most, the everyday life of the Chinaman.

Our view of the city was obscured by a series of sandstorms that increased in violence till the day of departure. Once more the cart road meandered across a monotonous plain. Here the sand flew, a perfect desert simoon. It curled up in drifts like snow. The mules coughed immoderately to clear their throats, while the rest of us helplessly drank it in at every pore. On the second day out we bade this confusion of sand, pork, and Mongol whirlwinds, farewell. It was mountainous and the scenery was charming from this to Teung-hwa-sung. We had every variety. Once or twice the mules were swept off their feet and almost carried away by the streams; then we would leave the rivers for winding avenues of trees; or, directly after being closed round by echoing crags, there would open before us some far restful view. We almost longed for the capacity of a Rip Van Winkle that we might doze off among such hills.

The less we saw of man, the cleaner, purer, and more delightful became our surroundings. There is a line in Korean sacred writing that reads,

Hanal arai sai, il man mulken kaondai sarami kajang qui hata (of all objects under heaven man is most precious). Looking at himself, one desires to feel that this teaching is true, but again taking a survey of others, he is inclined to doubt it. We all have an idea however, Koreans as well as Westerners, that man was originally this "precious object," but whether from ignorance or neglect, he now finds himself in a morbid, run-down condition, that even nineteenth century skill cannot diagnose. For this reason certain meeting house people discard the sacred writings and sing "every prospect pleases and only man is vile." Can such pessimism be true anywhere but in New England? True it is in North China as well; in fact it looks as though it were universally true.

We were not destined to escape the haunts of man for any great length of time, for one afternoon brought us out on the brow of a hill overlooking Teung-hwa-sung, sixty-five miles from the Yalu river. It is surrounded by mountains, and so seems entirely cut off from other thickly populated districts.

We stopped at Teung-hwa-sung for a couple of days to rest our aches and pains after the cart ride. Among other things, we were told of a party of Englishmen who had come through a year or two before, and how they had twenty horses and guns innumerable. Seeing so few accoutrements in our company, they shook their heads expressively, as if to say, England is not as powerful as she was a year or two ago.

I liked the inn-master in the place. Päk told me he was a Manchurian. It was said he understood Manchu writing, and that he was a distant relative of the present imperial line. He was oily enough, certainly, to have been anointed for a dozen kingships. This no doubt accounted for the proud way in which he sauntered about his own inn, and the dignity with which he behaved in general. He was kind to our whole party, to me in particular. He really seemed specially drawn to me. At night, too, he slept in our immediate neighborhood. Before retiring he would shed a few of his outer garments, skillfully going round the seams of these with his teeth, biting in every nook and corner. If the objects of his displeasure were specially numerous, he would engage his grandson to search for him, and the lad's success could be noted by the sound of the victims cracked on the dining table. A most remarkable old man! But like all others we had to bid him farewell and start from Teung-hwa-sung.

We still recall the morning of our departure. Cart number two had started ahead, and by some mishap was upset. Mr. Sö was ejected, as if shot from a catapult, but after feeling of his headdress and person in general, said no harm was done. It was not far from Teung-hwa-sung, that we met two old wayfarers, each carrying a bundle and a heavy club. A sudden misunderstanding arose between them and our cartmen, over what we have never been able to understand. They talked together for a few minutes in an animated way without coming to any conclusion, and then armed with clubs all round, went for one another. There were no striking of attitudes and tableaux, such as we see in Korea, but good hard fighting with blows that echoed. It was refreshing indeed, for it taught us that there was life still in the Far East. We viewed it from our reserved seats in the cart, not without anxiety lest these tawny wayfarers should kill our cartmen, and leave the further education and bringing up of the mules on our hands. They fought so desperately that Păk and Sö climbed out to the rescue, and then it looked as though Koreans and all might perish. It was only upon the entrance of "foreign-devils" upon the scene, that peace was finally restored. That same evening I made signs of inquiry to our cartman as to the general state of his health. He replied by trying to lift his right arm. When by dint of effort he got it to the horizontal, his expression of suffering reminded me of a face in an old copy of Dante's Inferno.

With such variations to season our journey, we left the clearings behind and entered the forest. On the outskirts we passed a number of coal-fields that showed some signs of life, but otherwise it was nearly all a wilderness. There was an inn in the pine forest to which the carts took us, but beyond there was only a footpath. It was twenty miles from the Yalu, and as there was no coolie market to draw from, we had each to turn in and shoulder a bundle. It was April nineteenth, but in the shaded cañon through which the path led the ice was still seven and eight feet thick. That afternoon we came upon a wretched Chinese family, moving, they said, to Ma-er-shan, a place near the foot of the Ever White Mountains. Their horse had fallen over a precipice and had scattered their few provisions and utensils everywhere. A poor woman, with several half-frozen children, was looking on helplessly at the disintegrated pony.

After ten miles that seemed twenty, we found a Korean hut, and, to our delight, dined on rice and *kimch'i* (pickle) once more. Here lived one of the many squatters that we find beyond the Yalu. These people look more prosperous and contented there than in their native Chosön. This strip of land was formerly neutral territory, but is now in the hands of the Chinese.

We slept peacefully, feeling as though we were home after our wanderings. Chinamen called to inspect us, but they never seemed to agree as to just what we were. One little boy carrying a pipe found his way in likewise. This pipe he coolly filled, and lit, and sat down to smoke before us. I inquired his age. Păk said he was five, though he did not look more than four. Never having seen as young an urchin indulging in the art of tobacco smoking I asked Păk if he would sell his pipe. He said "No!" Păk inquired again, and then young Manchuria began to cry, saying that he would not sell his pipe for anything; in which case we would not insist. About this time his father came in, and hearing of the proposal that had been made, held a consultation with his son. When they had considered the question on all sides, Manchuria, junior, offered it to Păk for twenty cents. We gave the price even though the onlookers did smile and say you could buy a new one for less than that. We bought it, I say, and we keep it now as the pipe of the smallest boy in the world who can smoke and not get sick.

This day took us to the Yalu once again, though smaller than at Eui-ju, still a swift and powerful river. Our crossing was at a lumber camp where several hundred Chinese coolies were hewing timber. Immense logs, four and five feet in diameter, had been floated down the Yalu, and were here cut up and carried inland. Our entrance was a signal to stop work. They gathered round us, not a very orderly looking group, and their laughter and wonderment was not of a cultured kind. Pāk said they wanted eight dollars to scow us over the river; and when he told them that we carried passports, issued by the almighty government of the Celestial Empire, these celestials merely grinned, saying they feared no law and were responsible to no empire. Pāk said he would give no more than fifty cents if we waited there till New Year, so there was nothing for the rest of us to do but to wait on Pāk. An hour or so later, he returned, having in some mysterious way completely won the victory, for they scowed us over for nothing—Pāk making them a gift of our few remaining Chinese cash. It seems to me it requires as much good sense and skill to manipulate a Chinese lumber camp, as it does to settle a fishery question or manage a political party.

It was the same Pāk that came home to Korea some fifteen years ago, teaching doctrines about resurrection of the dead and eternal judgment, so that his superior put him in the lockup and paddled him that he might sin no more. Păk's only answer in his far north dialect was, "You may paddle me but you surely cannot stop my speaking." Long live Păk!

That afternoon we sat on a mountain pass and took a last farewell of the lumber camp, the mountains round about, and the winding Yalu.

IV

FROM POVERTY TO RICHES

It was a fierce winter day. I had ridden some forty miles across the plains that end in a stretch of mountains separating East and West Korea. It was part of a two weeks' journey, in which time I had been frost-bitten, snowed under, and last of all, had had to break a way through the drifts for seventy miles. The mountains seemed to have been buried neck deep, and the guide, with three coolies ahead, appeared and disappeared at the mercy of the snow. The little Korean ponies, noted for their sure-footedness, completely lost their heads, and I was shot into the drifts time and again, while the poor pony, off the track, would go down hopelessly into the depths, pack and all.

The five natives with me complained bitterly of the cold and of the wretched country through which we had been obliged to pass. They grew moody, as mortals do when weary; so we plodded on in silence, hoping to find a room in a village in the next ravine.

Korean huts at their best are noisome dens; at their worst as you find them in mountain villages, they are indescribable. A night passed in one of these has more soul-stirring horrors than all of Dante's vision. The wind that whistles over the plains, deals with you in a fierce, yet clean-handed way, but the atmosphere that enshrouds you at night, poisons your very lifeblood.

It was in the village of To'-Söng or Earthen Walls that we were to stop. In the dusk of the evening we wound down into it and put up at an inn, where I noticed an old man, partly barefoot in the snow, tottering in with two buckets of water. His shattered condition caught my eye—for Koreans, though they have but few earthly blessings, dress well and fare sumptuously. When I had a chance to talk with him, I found him a gentle spoken native, who as I learned afterward, carried under his ragged dress a tender heart and manifold experiences of want and suffering.

He had walked four hundred miles from his home in Kapsan up to the capital which he had seen for the first time. He had thought to get work and to increase his little money, but the undertaking had proven a failure. With his money spent and the residents of the capital looking askance at a feeble old northerner, he had to turn homeward, and, working his way slowly, had reached To'-söng, a quarter of the distance.

I tried to draw the old man out in order to get a glimpse if possible of the inner self of one who possessed so little of the world's goods. He was simple and childlike in his manner, and asked respectfully for my "honorable country." I told him I had come over the sea from away beyond everywhere to tell Koreans about the God who made the world, and who certainly loved them. He confessed that he was not as anxious about the life to come as he was about a little meat and drink and a few yards of plain clothing for this present world. I liked his honesty, for it is so easy to find a pious oriental with full stomach and warm suit, all of which is due to a hardworking woman, proclaiming himself not of the earth earthy.

Nam, for that was his name, did not seem in the least afraid of me, but sat chatting in the doorway, his deep hungry eyes and hollow cheeks telling his story of earth's pilgrimage. As I sat waiting for the evening meal I gave him a few cash, with a hint that I would be grateful for any assistance he could give me against the unseen armies of the night. The old man looked carefully about him, and then, with a precision that did my heart good, took the worth of several such strings of cash out of one or two disreputable insects that happened to be careering along the wall of the room. I date this point as the beginning of a friendship, which I hope may last many a year.

The supper was brought in steaming, and smelling of pickle, soup, and stringy looking meats—usually called "dog" by foreigners who have never tasted of them. It was a welcome odor, and as I took up the chopsticks, Nam wished me a "mighty dinner" and withdrew. What were the old man's thoughts I know not, but if he had no greedy longing in his heart for my lot, I should say he was not far from the kingdom—as an Oriental so situated would naturally speak flatteringly, while thinking, "see the foreign dog devouring the best of the land, while I, a child of ancestral promise, go hungry!"

In the course of time the supper odors and the musty room faded away, the dogs grew quiet, the ponies under the eaves ceased their munching, and with gates barred and doors pulled tight, we slept; Nam to be free from want and poverty, and I to dream of a happy home awaiting me after the mountains and storms of the journey: in miniature a picture of a longer pilgrimage, and the Home of Light, awaiting all who trust in The Light of Life.

I slept, baked almost brown by the frying-pan floor. This floor, by the way, is the delight of every truly Korean heart, and in no particular does our barbarian nature seem to them more hopelessly depraved, than in our antipathy for their ways and means of sleeping.

As usual, the Koreans were up at first cockcrow, about 1:30 A. M., feeding their ponies in preparation for an early start, as they say, at about seven o'clock. There was a constant noise,—the cutting of straw, the dipping and pouring of water, the crackling of fires, and the flup-flup of the ponies' lips, in their efforts to get a few beans from the bottom of a trough of water. Old Nam was up and hard at it. Had he not been a Korean I should never have forgiven him for such an unseemly uproar. I used to tell Koreans that two hours' feeding was sufficient to prepare any pony for a journey of fifteen miles, and that time spent above this was labor in vain, disturbing the peace of the household, and wearing out the patience of the pony; but it had just as much effect, as if I had requested the fowls perched above my door to desist from immoderate crowing. Brute force is the only earthly power I know of that will stop either Korean natives or fowls from going persistently along the way of their ancestors. Cockcrowing is something that I took but little note of at home. In fact, since the introduction of clocks and watches, our fowls have, I think, lost the art. But Korean birds, with all the field to themselves, have gone on vying with each other for the last three thousand years, until now their crowing has attained a perfect steam-whistle pitch.

Such were the surroundings of old Nam the morning following our first acquaintance. A fire of pine knots lighted up the quadrangle within the low thatched roofs, showing the ponies with long lips and dejected countenances, dogs growling and shivering, the proprietor with towsy head looking on, and Nam, the moving figure in the picture, busy at his work.

I told him, among other things, that if ever he should pass Gensan in his wanderings please to call on me, and if I happened to have work on hand, I would be glad to help him to it. After breakfast he led my pony out, helped me to a comfortable seat in the pack, and then, with profound bow and many thanks, saw me off.

I was to be home in two days. This was inspiration enough to carry me unconsciously over the range of mountains; and on the second day, after various mishaps and good fortunes, I started out of Nam-san on foot, a short distance in advance of my ponies. To go afoot in Korea, is to call down upon your head the contempt of the multitude. And yet, when it suits best my convenience, I intend to go afoot, even though it be to the utter confusion of my best native friends. At the time I mention, I was passing through a quiet grove of trees, feeling how strange and wonderful it was that I should be blessed so far above old Nam and other poor mortals. A sort of kindly feeling had settled over me for Koreans in general, when, at a turn in the trees, I was suddenly accosted by two portly-looking, swellish gentlemen, who in the lowest possible terms, asked me what kind of beast I was, where I had been stabled, and whither I was hoofing it. My blood was up at once, and I asked them the reason for thus stopping me. This seemed to heighten the joke in their eyes, and furnish them with fresh material for mirth. I did not feel quite willing to honor them with righteous anger, and yet this was clearly a case where something must be done. So before he was aware, I took a gentle grip of the neck folds of the chief speaker's coat, and said: "Gentlemen, it is a fact, you may talk to me thus with impunity, for I am a soft and gentle mortal, but," tightening my grip the while, "if you talk like this to other westerners, they will certainly reply thus,"—at which I brought down my oak cane, and repeated the blow in such a way as to take every atom of dust out of those far-Eastern trousers. The second gentleman, evidently convinced by the demonstration, moved quietly away. The one in hand begged my pardon as a "great man" (tă-in), and confessed that he had no idea that I was the refined and cultured gentleman that he now felt me to be. And so we parted, each of us having furnished the other with an item of experience.

A month and more had passed since my safe return home, when one morning my boy came to say that an old man had called and wished to see me. I asked him in, and who should it turn out to be but Nam. He had put on a less ragged coat over his tattered garments, which so improved his appearance that he looked at me as though life were still full of promise. He had come to see and to thank me, and to find whether I had some work that he could do. I had wood to split, and roots to dig, shortly, and so we entered into contract—Nam to work for me, and I to pay him as I thought best. He was so gentle and mild that I feared the sticks would suffer but little at his hands; and yet not so, for with tobacco enough to lend him inspiration, he faithfully executed the tasks assigned. I can see him still, as he was in those days of his adversity, his gentle face set against that wood pile, and can hear his soft tones asking my advice about the work.

I have a native assistant who is built after the plan of an Egyptian taskmaster. He invariably regards gentleness of manner as a sign of lurking deceit, and anything like softness of speech he abhors. He eyed Nam, somewhat in the way a thistle might look down upon a milkweed, feeling certain that the latter would come to no good end, and accused him of uttering falsehoods in his hearing. "He says," protested my assistant, "that he has a home up north, cows, and fields, and sufficient to live on, and now he wants to make a little money so as to buy a few clothes and go back looking decent. The idea of an old offspring of that kind talking about owning cows." "Wait and see," I said, "don't condemn the old man so hastily;" but his mind was like a millstone, and Nam henceforth stood condemned.

Two months passed, and he was still with us, little better in appearance, it is true, for he was saving his extra cash together with the clothes we gave him. He seemed happy, and every morning sat in the doorway listening to the Bible-story of sin and death and ransom. We tried to make it plain, and though seeming to fail, we trusted that God would open his heart to receive it. He thought it very wonderful that God should speak so plainly—that He should have come down to earth, and have lived, and been poor, and, stranger still, should have offered himself a sacrifice for us all.

He was quite a farmer in his way. He taught me how to plant pines and willows. Said he "Plant the large end of the limb and you get a common willow; reverse it, plant the small end and you get a weeping willow; which idea I found to be interesting even though it did not prove actually true. He managed the gardening, took care of the flowers, and would search out a bug or thieving insect with great success. He informed me one morning that a certain creature, something in the form of a mosquito (mo-gi), was after our strawberry plants. My wife's interest in strawberries had never flagged, even through whole seasons of bare vines, so I said "My wife would be glad, I know, if you could capture that bug." He came a few mornings later, saying that he was happy to report to me that he had risen before daybreak and caught that mosquito, and that now we might expect strawberries in the near future.

Another morning, all unexpectedly, the old man came to say that, now the snow was gone, he would have to go back to see how his home was in the far north (Kapsan). I told him how sorry we would be to have him go; but it seemed best, and Nam came with his new white overcoat on to bid us peace and farewell. I saw wrapped away in his little bundle of earthly possessions a few tracts and parts of the New Testament. Did he know the secret of these as we hoped and prayed? With many expressions of thankfulness, the worn face disappeared, and the gentle spirit in its plebeian dress had gone and left us.

A man's place in life is not always to be judged by what he owns or by the cut of coat he wears. Sometimes people that own nothing, and wear any kind of coat that is given them, have eyes that stir our souls, and lines in their faces that move to tears. A tender soul looking out inquiringly or trustingly from its earthly windows, is worth meeting in a world so full of hardness, and hatred, and cast-iron perfection.

The summer wore round. Four months had passed away, when on a certain afternoon, a well-dressed figure with fresh lacquered hat came in at the gate, and turned toward my room. The face I knew, but there was something strange. Why! yes, it was Nam, all dressed up 'tis true, but just as gentle and respectful as ever. I said, "Why, friend Nam! Is it peace? How comes it?" He first inquired for my wife and little girls, and then told me how he had been home, and was now returning with two of his cows to sell in the Japanese market. Two cows to sell! Why I could not have been more surprised if he had told me he was a millionaire; and yet he did not look at me proudly. I saw he could be great, and not be ruined: something so little seen on earth. I told him how glad I would be to have him call often while he stayed, and offered him a seat, which he declined out of respect to me. My Egyptian assistant was as surprised as if the angel Gabriel had met him. He tried to reconcile this with human nature in general. I doubt not he searched the Chinese classics to find if it were possible for gentleness and humility ever to keep company with prosperity and earthly possessions. Yang said to me "I thought Nam So-bang was false, but he is true, every inch of him; in fact he is a wonderful old man." I went out to where he had his cows tethered on the hillside to see him. One was a red cow, the other brown, both in good condition. A few days later he sold them to the Japanese for forty-five dollars.

It was the first time I had ever seen a man of the people with no debts and so large a supply of cash on hand. The Egyptian and his associates were speechless. I suggested that they might do well to *kow-tow* (bow down) before so worthy a Korean as Nam, for as for me, I had seldom seen his like.

One more interview. As he was leaving for his home he came to ask for four of the books that told about Jesus They had read what he had taken before, and now he wanted a New Testament each for three families, and one for his own. He said they could read the Chinese characters in these homes, and besides, he would tell them what he himself had heard about salvation.

We told Nam that we would never forget him, and my wife joined me in wishing him peace on his journey—the peace that passeth understanding.

V

THE KOREAN PONY

Among the creatures that have crossed my path, the one that has had the most influence on my personal character is the Korean pony. It would be impossible to recount the varied experiences through which he has led me. Instead of lifting my hand and pointing to some noted professor or eminent divine, as the master spirit of my life, I stand a safe distance off, point to the Korean pony, and say, "He has brought more out of me than all of the others combined." In his company I have been surprised at the amount of concentrated evil I have found in my heart; again, as he has carried me safely along the dizziest edge, I could have turned angel and taken him upon my back.

My usual pony has been, not one of your well-groomed steeds from the palace stables, but a long-haired, hide-bound one, for which your whole heart goes out in pity. "Weak creature," you say, "how easy it would be for him to expire." But after a little experience of his company you change your mind; for you find his heels are charged with the vitality of forked lightning, and that upon slight provocation he could bite through six inch armor-plate. Experience has taught me to treat him carefully, as you would an old fowling-piece loaded to kill, and in danger of going off at any moment.

Korean ponies hail principally from the southern island of Quelpart, from the group off the west of P'yöng-an, and from Ham-Kyöng province. A Manchu breed is being introduced of late, but they are more bulky, harder to feed, and not nearly as good roadsters.

The breeding districts are under charge of officers named *Kammok*. They have with them keepers, who twice each year, lasso a certain number of ponies and send them to the palace. There they pass their palmy days. When their hair grows long and they take on a sheep-like look, they are turned out through the back gate and become pack-ponies, carrying goods along the four main roads of Korea. They keep this up until they develop ringbone, spavin, rawback, windgalls and heaves. Then they are bought by a Korean living near the "New Gate," and for the remainder of their mortal existence are used specially to carry foreigners. The fact that the animal is dangerously ill, and the risk so much the greater, accounts for the double charge made to all foreigners by the man at the "New Gate."

THE KOREAN PONY.

The Korean pony figures in literary and scientific ways as well. He is the animal of the twenty-fifth constellation, and appears specially as the symbolical creature of the seventh Korean hour (11 A. M. to 1 P. M.). This doubtless refers to the fact that he eats his *chook* at that time, though 11 to 2 would have been a more correct division. We read also that his compass point is south. Probably the inventor of the Horary Table was on his way north at the time, and finding that his pony naturally gravitated the other way, marked it south. His poetical name is *tonchang* (honest sheep). While the noun here is well chosen, the adjective is purely fictitious, as we say "honest injun."

In size, when alongside of a Western horse, he looks like a ten-year-old boy accompanying his grandfather, or like an ordinary Japanese walking out with Li Hung Chang.

His gait is a peculiar pitter-patter, and rides very nicely until he reaches the raw-backed, spavin age, when he stumbles every few paces, calling forth remarks from the foreigner. The so-called Chinese ponies are all rough, awkward creatures. A pack on one of them heaves up and down like an old-fashioned walking-beam; while a Korean pony, in good condition, glides along like a palace Pullman. For a journey over such roads as we have, a small Korean horse will use up a large Chinese pony in less than three days, as I have found by actual experiment.

Their sure-footedness is a marvel. If you have been fortunate enough to escape the man at the "New Gate," and have really secured a good pony, then give him his way over all dangers of ice and precipice that you may chance to pass. Sit perfectly cool on your pack, for the danger is less when trusting to him than to your own feet. How my heart has risen to the occasion, and taken up its quarters in my mouth, as I have felt him glide along an eight inch path, overlooking a chasm with twelve feet of green cold water below. But never a failure, never once a slip. At such times, had I been in search of a joss to crack my head to, I should have enshrined my Korean pony.

And yet in spite of these excellencies my opening remarks are true, for in heart and soul he is a perfect fiend. Obstinacy is one of his commonest characteristics. He will have his own way as assuredly as any Korean coolie will have his. When the notion takes him, his neck is of brass, and his ideas fixed as the king's ell.

His diet is *chook* and chopped millet straw. *Chook* is boiled beans and rice chaff, and is fed to the pony in a trough of water. The beans are very few, the water very deep. The long lips and nose of the Korean pony is an evolution of nature in order to capture that bean in the bottom of a trough of water: he has been after it for generations. Another result is, the pony can breathe through his eyes while his nose is a foot deep in *chook* water hunting beans.

The fact that the water is always colored, leaves it uncertain as to the amount put in, and grievous are the disputations that arise over an equal division of these beans. On one of my journeys I had for groom (mapu) a huge-trousered, pockmarked fellow, whose disposition seemed to be to get into disputes and difficulties along the way. The pony I rode was a long nosed, dejected creature, that required three hours to feed. On one occasion I went out to hurry the animal up, and found it eye-deep in its trough, apparently having an extra good time. The innkeeper happening to pass by saw the twinkle in the pony's eyes, and concluded that the *mapu* had "squeezed" his beans. Immediately a most interesting drama was enacted, passing rapidly through the various acts of a tragedy. "To perdition, you and your beans," cries the *mapu*, meanwhile, currying his pony. With that, in a burst of tragic frenzy, the innkeeper seizing the brimming trough of *chook*, poised it in the air, and let fly at the *mapu*. With all the centrifugal force of a projectile, the trough grazed the pony's back and shot by the *mapu;* the water, taking the centripetal route, showered down over the head and shoulders of the innkeeper himself, the beans gliding gently down his neck. People speak of a horse-laugh, but a pony's smile is something that in watery richness of expression surpasses everything. That dejected looking pony smiled, and we resumed our journey.

They never allow the pony to drink cold water, "It is sure death," they say; neither do they allow him to lie down at night, but keep him strung up to a pole overhead by ropes, so that the creature is perfectly helpless, and all the roosters of the village warm their feet on his back and crow the place into a perfect pandemonium.

The work of feeding ponies, as I have before mentioned seems endless to one uninitiated. For a seven o'clock start in the morning you hear them up at half-past one slopping, dishing, crunching, jangling, wearying the life out of the miserable ponies. I begged and implored, but it was all in vain, for when a Korean pony and a native combine in some pet scheme, it is as useless to remonstrate as it would be to "pick a quarrel wi' a stane wa'."

By way of poetic justice, I love to see the pony shod—see him pinioned tooth and nail, bound head, feet, and tail in one hard knot, lying on his back under the spreading chestnut tree, with the village smithy putting tacks into him that brings tears to his eyes. But seasons like this are all too short to square up with him for the sins of his everyday existence.

To conclude by way of illustration: I was on a journey through the south, and had reached the city of Tagu, the capital of Kyŭng-sang province. There my pony took sick, and not being able to find one for hire, I asked one of the mayor of the city. The morning I was to leave he sent me round a perfect whirlwind of a pony. This was number one of a courier service, which necessitated changing horses every five miles. In the fourteen or fifteen animals that I enjoyed for the next three days, I had an excellent demonstration of the merits and defects of the Korean pony. As mentioned, the first horse was a great success, the next one also was in good condition and fairly well proportioned. On mounting, however, I found he had a peculiar gate. A limp that defied all my efforts to locate seemed in fact to possess his entire being; a jerking that left one's inmost soul in shreds. The inconvenience of this five miles was indescribable. Taken all-in-all, he was the most uncomfortable horse I have ever had anything to do with. Glad was I to hand him over at the next post-house. Pony number three was soon in waiting. He carried me out of the yard brilliantly. The road skirted the bank of a river. A magnificent view, thought I, and a pleasant pony to ride on; when suddenly he stopped, reversed all his ideas and began backing at a dangerous pace directly for the edge. I managed to get off just in time to save myself, and then, thinking to teach him a lesson by a good shaking up, attempted to assist him over the side. But no! he skillfully grazed the edge at an angle sufficient to have dumped anything from his back, and righted himself again as neatly as though he had done it a thousand times. Evidently, it was a scheme on his part to take my life. I tried him, found him guilty, and sentenced him to as many lashes as the whalebone in my possession would mete out. I used it up—the only thing in all my personal effects that the natives admired—and then, on the advice of Mr. Yi, decided to walk till the landscape was a little less picturesque. When we had left the river and gained the open fields, I tried him again, thinking surely that his spirit must be broken by this time. But it was not long till the old sensations took him, and he was again backing up at terrific speed. As there was no immediate danger, I thought to let him back, which he did until he had run me into a bristling shrub, that lifted my hat off, combed me up generally, and marked my face. Having no more whalebone I gave him up entirely, and footed it for the remainder of the distance.

Then came three indifferent animals that just managed to make their five miles. Mr. Yi, in every case, gave special orders to provide good horses, and the answer of the post-house keeper was invariably so bland and righteous like, that I could have seen him caned, knowing how little these answers meant. After one of the most immaculate keepers on the whole way had professed to have gotten an excellent pony, we again moved on. When the creature was far enough away from the stable to protect his master from any assault on our part, he lay down peacefully in the middle of the road. There he remained until lifted bodily by tail and ears, and then he refused to put his feet squarely on the ground, Mr. Yi and the two pony boys straining themselves to the utmost to hold him erect.

The last one that I felt particularly incensed against, was a ragged looking beast that was troubled with a weakness in its fore quarters. Without the slightest provocation he was all the time going down on his nose, his hinder parts, however, keeping perfectly erect. If his strength could have been more equally divided fore and aft, he might have made a passable pony; but as it was, no forelegs at all would have been the only honest turn-out. The creature hobbled along, kept me in a state of constant suspense, played on my hopes and fears most cruelly, and at last, in an utter collapse, pitched me clear over his head, to the total destruction of my personal appearance.

VI

ACROSS KOREA[1]

DURING the past eight years it has been my misfortune, shall I say, to have crossed the peninsula of Korea twelve times, by different roads, and at different seasons of the year. No other American or European having had such a varied experience of the crossroads of the hermit kingdom, I have thought it a subject upon which I might venture to write.

Korean historical associations are connected with the far north. Keui-ja, who was a sort of Christopher Columbus and George Washington combined, crossed the Yalu, bringing civilization and deliverance with him. The Puynites, an interesting race, who gradually overran the peninsula, lived at the foot of the Ever White Mountain, which still stands, like a silent sentinel, on guard against Russia. All the old tales of heroes and marvellous mysteries gather about the far north; and it was in the hope of verifying some of these that I resolved to make a trip from Manchuria knowing that no Westerner had yet penetrated eastward from the Yalu through the region that I most desired to see.

[1] Written for the Yokohama Literary Society.

There were seven of us in the party, five Koreans and two Americans, who, in the month of April, crossed the river three hundred miles from its mouth, about midway between the forty-first and forty-second parallels of latitude, and started eastward.

The river, here some three hundred yards wide, is swift and powerful, and we should never have been able to cross, but for a yellow-faced opium-smoking Chinaman, who, after nearly half-a-day's parleying, agreed to let us have his boat.

After a walk over abrupt hills covered with birch, beeches, and pines, we came suddenly upon the Korean town of Chásöng situated in a valley on the bank of a river. It is built of low mud huts, with slabs of wood instead of thatch to protect from the rain. The inhabitants poured out with a rush, man, woman and child, to see what was coming. How so many white coats can assemble in so short a time, is one of the mysteries that we never try to solve in Korea. One long, lanky fellow, to the amusement of the crowd, made a sort of hunchback nod at me and said, "Ugh! what are you?" We took a step or two toward him, and gave a look to signify that we were from the cannibal islands. At once he was polite, and all his companions fell into line. They were exceedingly kind and gave us the best they had in the way of fare; but to the last, I really believe they did not know whether we were men or evil spirits—never having seen a Westerner before.

The natives were dressed, as elsewhere, in a white suit made up of huge baggy trousers and padded jacket. For headgear they wore a horsehair band, keyed so tightly that every line of expression was stretched out of the face, with scarcely enough muscular freedom for the eyes to close. The whole was surmounted by a broad-brimmed, gauze hat, whose duty is not to shade the head, but to cage off that precious badge of citizenship, the topknot. The most overwhelming part of a Korean's dress is his trousers. When worn they are not so surprising; but when seen on a clothes-line or stretched on the grass to dry, they are simply prodigious. I might say, that in width, an ordinary Korean's pantaloons would amply cover the nakedness of the largest Buddha in the far East, or provide a loose undergarment for the Statue of Liberty, New York harbor.

We were doomed to disappointment in this town, as one so often is when travelling in Korea. It seems that the ferryman overdrank himself that night and let his boat float away from under him. The next morning it was fast to a rock, half submerged in the middle of the river, and we were informed that the way was closed against us to the Ever White Mountain. We sent a note, with a present, to the magistrate requesting him to rescue the boat and help us along. His reply was that he would do so at once. Six hours later when we visited the spot to see how matters were progressing, we found a noisy group on the bank wrangling at the top of their voices, a perfect fight all round, the boat meanwhile fast to the rock mocking us from the middle of the river. The result of it all was that they took the ferryman to the *yamen*, fastened him down face to the ground, and gave him thirty blows with a paddle large enough to break a man's back. This they said was in accordance with Korean law, and was done out of respect for us. Next morning our party had to wade the cold green water which, along with the humiliating sensation that the magistrate had tricked us out of the boat, and that the poor ferryman had been beaten on our account, was depressing.

The Korean system of bridging streams is one of the strangest in existence. The natives are amazed beyond expression at the idea of a bridge standing all the year round, so up come their bridges at about the first of June, only to be replaced at the close of September. They say it is because of the rainy season, but the longest rainy season I have known has not exceeded a month and a half. I rather think it is because of the idea of personality that they associate with the bridge as with so many other things. Feeling that he should have a rest with the summer season, they pile him up by the roadside and let him bask and snooze in the sun, in order that he may set his limbs the more firmly for his task of spanning the stream through the winter.

These bridges, at best, are only about four feet wide, with a flooring of pine brush and earth resting on poles planted in spans of eight feet. To ride over this on the top of a pack pony, and to feel it giving under your feet like a patent spring mattress, creates a sensation of expectancy in one not unlike that produced by a Yokohama earthquake.

Usually the natives are willing, for a few *cash*, to carry one on the back over unbridged streams, but on this northern trip I was specially unfortunate. I came upon a mountain torrent, not deep, but sufficient to cover the boot-tops, and just on the bank met a stout, bare-legged coolie, leading a horse. Said I, "You'll help me now, over this bit of water, please?" He looked at me with unspeakable contempt and replied, "Get yourself over." As I had never before met such an independent coolie I was quite startled. "But I'll pay you, my good man!" "None of your pay for me," said he, and proceeded to walk away. Not that I would be intentionally impolite to a coolie, but the inspiration of the moment in some way caught me, and I was onto his back tighter than the Old Man of the Sea. He muttered to himself threatenings, then proceeded slowly, stopping to reconsider in the middle of the stream, but it was hopeless, so he landed me safely. I apologized and expressed the hope that we might still be friends, adding some extra pay by way of indemnity. He however stood looking at me in speechless amazement—is standing so yet for ought I know.

We now struck a region of absolute destitution. It is true we saw beehives here and there, but could get no honey. There was nothing but millet and wild onions—no rice, no chickens or meat of any kind; and boiled millet is like so much sawdust in hot water. Our bundles too, seemed to grow heavier, and we could find no additional means of transportation, excepting two extra coolies, whom we hired. A young fox-terrier, like ourselves, grew thinner every day, refusing to eat millet. The only thing he would eat was a sticky candy made from sorghum seeds, one variety of which actually pulled his teeth out and left his mouth bleeding, so that it was with difficulty we got him through alive.

Among the grains of the far north we found Barbadas millet (*sorghum vulgare*), having red seeds, also panicled millet with seeds of a grey color. These varieties are sown on damp lowlands in drills, and the yield is claimed to be two hundredfold. The distribution of these grains is general throughout Korea. I have found them about Fusan, in the south, as well as on the Chinese border. Common millet, having a yellow grain, is sown in drills on dry land. Its yield is also very large, and most of the northern inhabitants subsist upon it. Buckwheat is also grown in the valleys, and is used in the preparation of vermicelli, the most popular dish in Korea. Beans, peas, barley, oats, wheat and maize are also grown in small quantities. Oats and potatoes Koreans particularly dislike.

One evening after a weary tramp, we called for something to eat at a small cabin, and the old dame in charge, said with a long face, she had nothing in the world but oats. This was a welcome sound to us after millet, so we ordered some boiled. But the Koreans of the party declared that matters were getting worse and worse—for oats, they claim, will give one all the diseases in the catalogue. We each had our dish and turned in for the night. Toward morning, Sö, my Korean friend, who slept next me, was up and down groaning as though in great distress. "What's the matter?" I inquired. "I have an attack of 'summer complaint,'" said he. The day before we had walked ten miles through a fall of snow, and I could hardly understand how he could have an attack of "summer complaint." "Those oats," said he, "have done it."

Sleeping in a small Korean hut I found, at first, to be one of my hardest trials. In a tight room, eight by eight, by six, without one particle of ventilation, the floor heated nearly to the frying point, you spread your blanket. The inexperienced traveller, pursued by fiery dreams, baked almost brown, gasps for breath and wishes for the morning. But after a year or two of practice, one gets to like the hot floor, for as the natives say, it lets you out after a cold day's journey.

The homes of the gentry (*yangban*) are usually very neat and attractive, the rooms well papered and clean; but the inns and huts in which we lodged on this northern trip were certainly far from comfortable. There is an oppressive odor common to a Korean room, that took me months to analyze. It seemed to prevail in large quantities everywhere. I found at last, that it was composed of two ingredients, one from the castor-oil lamp that sputtered in the corner, the other from a row of festering bean-balls hanging from the ceiling. After gathering the dust and cobwebs of a winter, these bean-balls are placed in water till fermentation begins, then the liquor is strained off and boiled into *soy*.

Because of this sleeping room, life was a burden, until a friend of mine invented a special dress that serves as a coat-of-mail. It is a huge sack, with smaller bags for the arms, and a draw string at the neck. Clad in this panoply of war, you turn on an American invention, which we call a gatling gun, and scatter insect powder over your face, neck, and pillow. This insures sleep. But until these modern inventions were introduced, the nights were passed with what waging of war, what slaughter, what muttered imprecations. But there is still another danger that neither coat-of-mail nor patent insufflator can protect from, and that is disease. As an illustration: on one of my last trips across Korea, after a cold day's journey, I spread my blanket on the floor of an eight foot square room that opened into another of the same size. When I was comfortably located for the night, I was disturbed by sounds of moaning from the room into which mine opened. It was so darkened that I could not see clearly, but I made out two children covered with a quilt. I asked the grandmother in charge what was wrong with them. Her reply was "His Excellency the spirit of smallpox is with us," and she hastened to make her evening sacrifice of rice cake. No other house being available, nothing remained but to sleep the night in company with this unclean spirit. However, no harm came of it. As in so many other cases in the East, the Great Spirit of Safety seems to accompany one through exposure and dangers that we would never dream of at home.

Yet I do not think Korea objectionable. To me it is the most attractive country in the world. The climate is good; the people, a dignified, trustworthy, kind-hearted race; their language and ancient customs most interesting. Natural beauty abounds. The hills and streams are alive with pheasants, wild duck, geese and turkeys. Herds of deer too, come cautiously down into the valley to feed, and above all, are frequent announcements of the regal presence of the tiger.

But to continue our journey. We noticed a succession of tiger traps, such as Koreans build from logs and stones, with a door that falls on the entrance of the tiger. But tigers are too cunning to enter a trap readily. We had proofs of there being many of them in our immediate neighborhood. Their tracks showed that they journeyed by the same road we did. The first instinct of these animals seems to be to keep out of sight by day, so we seldom see them.

I remember what I thought was a huge grey cat once being brought into the room where I was sitting. Looking more closely I saw it was a young tiger. He turned over on his back, took my slipper in his mouth, kicked it up into the air, tossed it from him, and then pranced about as frisky as a kitten. I saw the same animal a year or so later, when he had grown to be a fierce caged brute that not even the man in charge dare approach.

Here also we found the land fairly well timbered with pines and hardwood trees, two and three feet in diameter, rarely seen elsewhere in Korea. Doubtless the time will come when this timber will be floated down the Yalu to some place where it can be put to good use.

We passed only one town of any size, a place called Huchang, and there we found our road again blocked to the Ever White Mountain. We were almost within sight of his grey top, but melting snows and spring floods made it impassable. We had hoped to reach the watershed of the Yalu and Tumen, but the road through the mountains was completely shut against us. So, full of disappointment, we were obliged to turn south.

The simple-hearted people in this town of Huchang knew nothing whatever of the world. The magistrate came to call, bringing a live chicken or two by way of a propitiatory offering. It was then about noon, and he asked what time of day it might be in our honorable country.

"Nighttime," we replied. He gave a startled look. "What direction is your country from here?" and we pointed him toward the centre of the earth. He caught hold of something to steady himself from the shock this gave him, and inquired if we lived underground. When we told him that the world was round and that we lived on the other side, we transcended the pale of his interest; so he changed the subject, and bade us go in peace as soon as possible.

Here were mountain streams and fairly good fishing. True, successful fishing is an art little understood by Koreans. They catch salmon and mullet during spawning season, and take fish, seasonable and unseasonable, whenever they can catch them. When we reached the east coast, we found nets hung on poles with long barriers that serve as drives stretching out to them, cabled fast to the shore by strands of peuraria creeper. These nets hang for some five months of the year. They are intended specially for herring, but they take also cod, tai, skate, flounder, sole, turbot, thornback and poisonous globe-fish. But it is an indolent kind of fishing that yields little profit. The only success the fishermen have is up north, beyond the forty-first parallel of latitude, in catching pollack. This fish, not unlike a small cod, is taken in great quantities, dried, and shipped to all parts of the country, supplying a cheap and wholesome article of food.

We left Huchang and started south. Gradually the country grew less and less wooded, until nothing but scrubby pines were to be seen. The third day out, we came upon a mining town with smelting furnaces. Here they were separating copper from the ore, and shipping it by pack ponies to P'yöng-yang, to be minted into cash. The mining industry in Korea is in the crudest state imaginable. They dig gold only from the alluvium, making no attempt to disturb the mountains, because they are all sacred. On the fourth day we came upon gold diggings. My companion and I asked a weather-beaten miner to wash us out a sample. Squatting down on the edge of the stream, he filled his wooden basin with water, rocked it back and forth until at last he had washed all the mud over the edge, and there lay three or four specks of gold barely visible to the naked eye.

It had taken two ponies to carry our traps at the start; when these failed us, four coolies could just manage; now we reached a point where neither ponies nor coolies were to be had. We induced a farmer to let us have his two cows for a consideration, but the packs proved too heavy, so he gave the job up. As there were not three cows to be had, we were left hopeless, in a wretched inn, full of all uncleanness. I remember well my sojourn at that inn, as I had both cheer and discouragement liberally dealt out to me. The old grandmother asked if I had any good books with me. "Why no," I said, "we have given them away long ago; but where did you ever hear of a good book?" "Oh!" she cried, "I know of the Western Book, and I know westerners are good people, and that they have not come to harm us." This was encouragement, like rain on thirsty ground, after being pointed out for weeks as foreign devils, etc. The good old dame quite won my heart. Of the old man however I was less sure. Feeling at home, I cast about for some amusement, and happily came upon a fishing rod and line. Why should I, a member of the family, ask permission to go fishing? So I took the rod, and was soon comfortably seated on a rock enjoying that delightful sport which, Dr. Johnson says, requires only a fly on one end and a fool on the other. Suddenly I felt a shock, not from a bite, but from a call behind me to bring home that fishing rod. I pretended not to hear; the storm would blow over in a little. Ah! yes, there was a most interesting bite now; but a whirlwind suddenly caught me, in which I lost line, fish, interest and everything. When I came to, an old Korean, seventy years of age, was carefully putting a fishing rod back in its place, while an American was pretending to dig wild onions on the bank of the river, the village people meanwhile looking on encouragingly.

But to return to my story. I said it was the baggage that kept us. We had one hundred and fifty miles still to go to the city of Ham-heung, which is on the east coast of Korea. How should we ever make the distance? In answer there came by a mild looking native with a raw-boned cow bound for Ham-heung. Păk, a Korean of our party, asked this passer if he could devise some way of getting our boxes and blankets out of this wretched country. The native turned them over, and after due consideration, said he and his cow would take them all. "But," we protested, "two cows failed already; how can one, and a thin cow at that, possibly manage?" "My cow," said he, "can out-carry any two bullocks that travel these mountains." Morning came, and they piled up Crumple Horn, until she looked like some prehistoric monster on cow's legs. Steady as a ship, she got under way and plodded on to the amazement of us all, making thirty miles a day. Only on the last stage, when there were no beans to be had, did her faithful knees tremble, and we all felt deeply moved by the toil-worn expression in her brown face. A day or so after we reached home I called at the stable to see how she was, and found her peacefully dining off corn-stalks, with beans for dessert, scenting the evening air with her breath, as though her life had always been spent amid luxury and eternal pastures.

The night before reaching Ham-heung we passed in a miserable village near the summit of the mountains. They could get us nothing for breakfast but boiled potatoes and salt—rather a slim preparation for a thirty mile walk. It was the first of May and snow still covered the mountains. About ten in the morning we reached the summit, an elevation of some two thousand feet. Away to the east was the Sea of Japan, with a green summer valley lying between. The next hour's descent carried us from winter into a season of leaves and flowers. In Ham-heung there was abundance to eat; and how our party enjoyed beef and white rice once more, after weeks of starvation, I leave you to judge.

Thus prosaically ended our journey. We saw no remains of cities, no traces of fairy kings; met no special heroes, but the old man with the fish-pole. He belonged to the Puynite race, no doubt, or perhaps was some distant grandson of Keui-ja; but apart from him, all was a wilderness of bleak hills, low huts, tiger traps and millet.

VII

THE KOREAN BOY

The boy may be anything from fifteen to fifty-five years of age. He may be married or unmarried. He may even be male or female. He is the personal attendant of the Westerner and is *par excellence* the boy, or as they say in France, the *garçon*. He is the ever-present shadow, as visible in cloudy weather as in sunshine. He occupies the central place in the existence and history of all Western life in the Far East. As well expect a state to stand without a capital or a temple to flourish without a god as to find a foreigner and no boy. The boy is in fact the moving principle of his life. Nothing is done without sanction of the boy, and nothing that the boy vetoes can ever come to pass. The fact that the foreigner is helpless in his hand, inclines him to worship the boy as a little god, for nothing so calls forth adoration as tyranny wisely exercised.

It is a noticeable fact in Asia, that every Westerner has, in his immediate service, the best boy that has ever been seen. He does not stop to consider his own capabilities of choice, or his length of experience: his boy is perfect, and every other boy in the neighborhood is a disgrace to his employer. He knows not why they, who pretend to be missionaries, should keep such on their premises. He is thankful that he is not as other men are. His boy may rise with unwashed, greasy face, may mix bread with one hand and arrange his oily locks with the other, may accomplish a long list of imperfections, and yet the master will dilate on his excellence as boy. He is the god of the back kitchen, whose benign presence means life to the paleface in the inner room. He usually has another dirty little god or two to wait on him. These the American or European detests as a spirit worshipper detests *tokgabi* (goblins). He tells the boy so and orders their dismissal. The boy says *Nei-i-i* (very well), and keeps his little gods.

Like every other attending spirit, if you give the boy offense he leaves at once, and the crack of doom settles down over the unhappy head of his victim. Usually the boy comes back on increased pay and with less mercy than ever in his soul, and life moves on. We laugh at the Oriental's faithfulness to his cruel gods. He will fight for them even when their presence means death. Likewise, I have known Americans to threaten each other because one had spoken disparagingly of the frowzy-headed boy in the backyard, who was mixing germs and bacteria into dishes for the paleface to eat.

Like other inhabitants of the Orient, the boy understands the whole before you have taught him half, and always adds a touch of his own to give the needed completeness.

The Western wife is the one who reads deepest into the mysteries of the boy. He reveals himself to her because her demands, being greater than those of the bachelor, give scope and variety for his attainments. My wife was once involved in the preparation of a dinner to be given to the distinguished Western population of the city of Seoul, in the days when the whole company numbered less than the Knights of the Round Table. All the courses were safely under way and the kitchen was spread with the choicest dishes that those early days permitted. Canned vegetables, too, not so common there as in America, were called into requisition. "Open this can carefully, boy," said my wife, "and then heat the peas on the stove." "Heat the peas and then open the can," says the boy to himself, by way of touching off the order. My wife withdrew to the dining-room in the satisfaction of being at last ready for the guests. An Oriental bungalow is pretty; the brown woodwork and rafters, with light paper between, afford a pleasing combination when set with flowers and napkins and lighted tapers. Bang! went the kitchen, as though struck by a torpedo. There was a skirmish, and lo! dense darkness enshrouded the whole cooking paraphernalia. When the steam and particles of exploded peas had sufficiently settled to admit of entrance, the topknot of the boy was discovered issuing from behind the stove, while these words were heard, "Chosön boy no savez."

There were canned peas in every course that evening, to the confusion of my poor wife, but the story of their presence was accepted by the guests as more than compensation.

The boy was burned by the exploding can, and to this day cannot understand why it blew up, unless the devils were in it.

So the boy takes matters into his own hands. "I know," is his favorite motto (*amnaita*). He walks by faith in himself, and not by the sight of any mortal demonstration. He has unbounded confidence in his power to pilot a way through culinary complications. My wife had a kettle of catsup almost at a finish, the boy was plucking a chicken in readiness for dinner. "What is the red sauce for, madam?" asked the boy. "To be used with meat," said my wife; "for example, chicken." "Oh," said the boy, "*amnaita*" (I know). My wife returned to the kitchen a half hour later, and there was the chicken, submerged in the pot of catsup, boiling languidly, while the boy sat and expatiated to his dirty-faced satellites on the art of Western cooking.

The boy is full of resource; a situation that will baffle him entirely is hard to imagine. He will improvise a rope out of a few straws from the rice field, or build a comfortable saddle for you in the howling wilderness. His world is made up of the simplicities that belonged to the age of Adam; yet he can also take advantage of modern conveniences and methods, if need be.

The commissioner of customs paid us an afternoon call and we prevailed on him to remain for dinner. When my wife informed the boy that we would have him for our guest, he said, "We have nothing in the world for the great man; not bread enough, and no roast; we shall all die." My wife told him she would take no bread, and that canned meat would suffice for "potluck"; and as the commissioner was a considerate gentleman, there really was no occasion for any one to expire. "We shall all die," said he, "and go to perdition"—meaning that the honor of our house would fall. Dinner was served, the boy came sweeping in with the soup as though there were an abundant supply. Later we were awaiting the modest remnants of bread and canned meat, when the door swung on its hinges, and the boy, with an expression of oily radiance peculiar to the East, burst into the room with a roast of beef fit for Confucius. There was also bread enough and to spare. My wife sat asphyxiated. What could she do but accept a choice piece for herself, and express the hope that the commissioner would be helped a second time!

It was an eminent success as a dinner, but the question of where a roast was procured in a city destitute of Christian beef, and bread, where there are no bakers, was bearing hard upon her; yet it was not curiosity, but fear, that filled her soul. When we withdrew for coffee she asked in breathless suspense, "Kamyongi, where did you get the roast and the bread?" "Just sent to the commissioner's and said, 'The great man (*tăin*) will dine here, bring along anything you have cooked.'" With a look of mortification that was pitiful, my wife confessed then and there to the commissioner. He was an old hand in the East and the light of past days twinkled in his eye as he enjoyed to the full the joke of that most excellent dinner.

The boy is the guardian spirit of the paleface, notwithstanding the fact that he keeps him in torment. He will stand for his honor though he disturb a whole district in doing so. He has always been a source of fear to me lest he fall out with others on my account. He is a master-hand at discovering conditions uncomplimentary to those around him. "Boss," he would say to the innkeeper, "this is the thirteenth centipede I have killed on your veranda." "Indeed, where could they have come from?" says the innkeeper. "Have you bugs, too?" "None since I posted up those characters." "What is the name of this collection of pigpens anyhow?" asks the boy. "The name of our humble village is *Kămal*" (Dogtown), says the host. "I thought so," says the boy. This is a sample of the conversation, all of which was intended by way of doing me honor, proving how superior I was to my surroundings.

It is only fair to say that the average boy is trustworthy. He takes his "squeeze," which is as legitimate an operation in the Far East as the drawing of a salary at home. He expects to share in every variety of good fortune that befalls his master, without any thought of being dishonest; but there are of course questionable boys, as there are questionable people in every walk of life, and the following cases are cited to show the methods they adopt in deceiving their employer. The most afflicted person in this respect I have ever known was a Scotchman, who came East on a matter of business. He hired a boy to do his work, cook and care for him. This boy was to come every night, render an account of the day's expenses, and receive orders for the day following. Nothing palls on an impatient foreigner more than these visits of the boy with his book of Chinese characters; so the Scotchman would say, "Oh never mind, I'm tired to-night, come to-morrow." Several days would pass by, and then would come an evening of dire tussle and argument in a vain effort to straighten out accounts. "But," says the Scotchman, "I never ate forty eggs a day." "Oh yes! makee blead puddin', must have plenty egg," says the boy. The Scotchman was silenced, though not convinced. This matter of accounts grew more and more aggravated. There was heaped up against him a tremendous list of provisions— quantities of beef, mutton chop, ham, fruit, flour and eggs. Small portions of these to be sure he had eaten, but the meagre remnants that appeared for breakfast, tiffin, and dinner, were entirely out of proportion to the extravagant list of the evening. Resolved to investigate, the Scotchman dropped in about eleven from the office, to see what the supply looked like uncooked. He called the boy and asked what he had bought. "My buy good loast, one chicken, plenty thing." "Bring them in to me," said he. The boy disappeared, the Scotchman waited long and patiently. "Boy!" shouted he, but no answer. Determined to make an end once for all, he went into the kitchen and out to the back yard, and there was the boy plucking one of his favorite chickens, which he had killed in a desperate effort to make the supply tally with his account. He had meanwhile borrowed a piece of meat from a neighbor, and piled a few scraps on a plate, to which he called attention. The angry Scot caught the plate, and let fly, scraps, roast and all, straight at the boy's head. The concussion sent him spinning through the back gate, where he disappeared into a kind of nirvana, carrying the Scotchman's anathemas with him.

A second boy had been taught the necessary elements of his "pidgin," and the house was just beginning to get under way, when he announced the fact that he would have to go, as his mother was dead; but there was a boy that would take his place, "Number one, very good boy." "Never you mind," said the Westerner, "if you are determined to go I'll hire my own boy." "But I catchee more better, number one." Number one, he said, was the son of his father's half sister's cousin. "I don't care if he is the son of your great-grandmother, I'll have nothing to do with him," said the Scotchman. The boy went, but returned again; stood first on one foot and then on the other, hummed and hawed, and at last said, "There is a reason—" "Deed and I know it right well," said the Scot. "He give twenty dollar, catchee my place, now money all gone, no can pay back." The Scotchman's self-control had been worn down till his temper was poking through in holes. He could endure it no longer. With a mad rush he bundled the domestic through the rear gateway, adding something about him and all his heathen relations; and so he was again free to begin domestic life anew.

The boy of his own choice was now established in the kitchen and for a few days life flowed smoothly along. It was a new era in his existence. One morning in the most reasonable way imaginable the boy mentioned that he had some words he desired to say. "Say on then and be quick," said the impatient Aberdonian. "Master, makee buy one piece cow, catchee number one cleam." "Number one what?" "Cleam, good coffee." The boy at last prevailed, and the cow was bought. Then the boy was married, and took a native hut close by. He added an extra cow, from no one knew where, and pastured it in the master's flower garden. "Whose cow is this?" "That belong me," said the boy. "Take it out of my garden then," said the master. It soon developed that the boy was selling milk to the neighborhood—and the Scotchman on the whole commended him for his thrift. But the master's cream grew thinner every day, until nothing was forthcoming but blue malarial fluid. "Boy, I want cream, not skim-milk," said he. "All right, can do." Next morning there was an improvement, but just as he was enjoying his own cup of coffee there came a note from the consul's wife saying, "My dear Mr. Shand:—I fear your boy is putting water into the milk he brings us. Will you kindly see that this little matter is rectified." Confusion and sorrow were settling over the devoted head of the Scotchman. The herd of cows had now grown to six, pastured largely off his own ground, his only compensation being a few spoonfuls of cream for his coffee; but yet it showed the thrift of the boy, and thrift is something a Scotchman always worships. Next morning there was coffee and sugar in abundance, but no cream at all. "Boy! where is the cream?" "Master, very solly, to-day no have got cleam." "No have got cream and all these cows?" The boy explained that it had taken all he had to go round the neighborhood. "Confound it!" said the master, "I keep all these cows and get no cream?" Then the boy began to weep and said if he watered it, all the people said "no can do;" if he failed to give enough, they grumbled. Here he was, doing his duty, and every one was down on him, even his master. He would die. "But," said the Scot, "you idiot! What do you mean?" The boy said he wished he were dead. A day or two later complaints began coming in from people who had received no milk that morning—would Mr. Shand please see to it? The boy was called. "What about this wretched milk to-day?" "My no savez; my tell my wife look, see." "I have about made up my mind," said the exasperated Caledonian, "to be rid of both you and your cows." Next morning there was no milk for any one, and no breakfast for the Scotchman. His kitchen was as silent as the grave and as cold as Lapland. Where was the boy? Again there were letters from women on the verge of nervous prostration—"Sir: Do you intend to rob us of our supply of milk? We consider it very ungracious of you indeed." The Scotchman was a bachelor, and his blood was up. To think that this heathen should be the means of setting his lady friends against him was more than he could endure. He would horsewhip the brute, and hamstring his cows. When he reached the hut, he found the wife laid up from a beating she had received the night before for neglecting to milk; the boy had been arrested and was in jail for maltreating her; and the Scotchman was alone in the cold world, the fires of a purgatory burning hot within him.

The boy is really the executive officer of the state. He will solve a problem in bargaining or diplomacy that would baffle a native gentleman indefinitely. Never give the latter a task in either of these departments unless you desire it to be reduced to absolute confusion; but set the boy on the trail, yield him your confidence, and his devotion and executive skill will more than repay you. I have never yet heard of a boy's betrayal of a trust that was so imposed. His unwearied feet will cover long miles of distance in your behalf; his tongue will tell the wondering listeners your praises—how great you are, how wise, how generous, how rich, how glorious a master to serve. We have heard him speak so of others and sometimes of ourselves. Bless the boy! He will fight a whole town that calls you " barbarian "—as my own Yöngchuni did once when we entered a miserable raft of a place after nightfall. The people through the mouthpiece of a lanky mountaineer, said they had no stable room for savages. Quick as lightning Yöngchuni smacked him on the left cheek for his insolence. It was the touch of a button that piled all the loose population onto the prey like so many woolly dogs. Poor Yöngchuni he was the prey, buried out of sight, overwhelmed by violence, and all on my account. I was compelled to turn in and help him. How we survived, is still a mystery. As we moved ignominiously out of the place, I lectured him on keeping his temper. "But master they insulted you, how could I?" "But we must not fight." This reproof brought the tears, where the violence of the mob had but whetted him into anger. I told him I prized his faithfulness, pummelled as he had been. After thinking it over carefully and weighing the motives, I drew from it a profitable lesson for myself, and concluded that I would rather have fought like that on behalf of another, than have kept my temper for years.

I am given to understand by Orientals, that over-familiarity with any spirit brings disaster. This spirit may be necessary to material prosperity during the earthly pilgrimage, but it should never be made a companion of or spoken to in a loose or frivolous way. Keep it in its place, at a distance, and your house will flourish, your name will be great in the land. Never propitiate it in advance, but only on the appointed day, and then strictly in accordance with form. All of which rules apply in the case of the boy, and prove that if he be not a spirit or in league with spirits, he is in his being and characteristics like unto them, and so has power to bring joy and satisfaction, or to blast life and keep his victim in perpetual hot water.

VIII

KOREAN NEW YEAR

In their division of the year, Koreans, like the Chinese, prefer to follow the moon rather than the sun. Their confusion of the two reminds one of the Scotchmen, who when on their way home from market fell out and fought about the orb shining above them, one claiming that it was the sun, and the other that it was the moon. Neither being sufficiently steady of foot to settle it by actual war, they decided to leave the matter to arbitration, and asked a third party who was passing what he thought about it. After considerable time spent in balancing himself, he managed this reply, "I'm a stranger in these pairts, no vera weel acquaint, but it seems to me there's twa there, but whether sun or moon I canna tell."

I know of nothing that illustrates the Korean confusion of time and tide better than this story. His eye has been long rendered unsteady by superstition; and he stumbles along in his dim twilight thinking to himself that he is in full blaze of the sun.

At the close of the New Year season, that is on the night of the fifteenth of the first month, the Korean spreads his mat on the nearest bridge and bows three times to the moon, asking him for his light and guidance through the coming year. Each phase has been carefully watched for centuries, the quality and characteristics noted down, so that every fortune-teller in the land is full of the moon—of his good points, his dangers, his peculiar whims, just as a Briton understands his horse. When the Japanese were marching upon P'yöng-yang, I remember the Koreans saying that it was perfectly safe for China yet, as it was not a fighting moon.

And yet the ungrateful moon returns only evil for good. Every three years a moon is intercalated to fill up the deficiency in the lunar year. Once I remember this falling just at seed sowing, but not a Korean moved hand to sow his seed. When reminded that time was passing he simply said, "The intercalary moon is not reckoned in the season, we shall wait till it is over and then begin." The result was they sowed their seed a month late, and there was a famine in the land.

The noted moon of the year is the crescent that shines on the first night of the first month. Every native in the land feels that with it old things have passed away and that all things have become new. He pays his debts, puts on a new suit of clothes, bows his congratulations to the old men of the village, and has the younger men bow to him; and yet after it all, there is a lack and an aching void. He acts not unlike Job did, when he said, "Though I wash me with snow water and make my hands never so clean, yet wilt thou plunge me in the ditch and mine own clothes shall abhor me." Something dogs his footsteps of which he tries very hard to be rid; he calls in sorcerers, and fortune men, and during prolonged seances seeks their advice. A cook whom we left in Korea, had many times fallen a victim to a quarrelsome disposition, though he fought hard against it. We told him of the Christian way of combating such a foe, but it did not appeal to him. He said Koreans had a way too, but he would have to await the New Year for its trial. When the New Year came, late at night we found him in the courtyard flying a kite on which he had first written, "Evil disposition, impatience, bad words, street fights," etc. It was so dark that no kite could be seen; but when he had run the string out to its full length, he cut it and let it go, imagining that so he had rid himself of his enemies and could begin the year with new courage.

Another regenerating method commonly practised is to prepare a straw image which contains in its inmost being a written statement of one's sins and shortcomings, together with a few cash. On New Year's night beggars who play the part of scapegoat, come by asking for *cheyong* or the image. It is passed out to them, and they become possessed of the evil, selling their peace of soul for the cash within.

Again another method of finding peace, is by making offerings before a mountain shrine. We had one such in front of our gate, to which, among others, came an old woman to rid herself of her sorrows and burdens, carrying a chicken and a bowl of rice. It was a *live* offering, for she left the chicken tied by its foot to the tree. Its peepings brought our cook upon the scene, who cut the string, gave the bird shelter, and when the old woman came by again, said, "Mother! here's your chicken." But grandma lifted up her hands in horror, refused to take it, and warned him against what he would inherit—terrors worse than he had dispossessed himself of when he flew his kite.

The Korean is a marvel for mathematical calculations. "How much a mat?" I remember once asking a dealer. "Five hundred *cash*," was the answer. "Very well, I'll take twenty mats." "Never!" says he with indignation. "Cannot sell so many for less than six hundred a piece." Such reasoning is entirely inexplicable; betokening that mathematics have gone to everlasting destruction. His reckoning of age is also peculiar. It is not based upon revolutions of sun or moon, but upon the number of New Year's dinners partaken of, with an extra year thrown in, for what reason I have never been able to understand. Thus, if a child is born in December, and on New Year's day joins the family circle for refreshments, it is said to be two years old, though its actual existence may number only five or six days.

Though defective in mathematics, the Korean has other compensating excellencies. We have had a Parliament of Religions, at which we are glad he took no part; but when we shall have a Parliament of National Amusements, we hope to have him there flying his New Year's kite, for it is the one form of recreation in which he especially excels. At this season the upper air of the capital is alive with kites, dancing nimbly in groups or moving mysteriously here and there. His kite is small and square without wings or tail, and its evolutions are marvellous. In fairly calm weather a skillful flyer can command an arc of some ninety degrees with his kite. By a turn of the wrist and a sweep of the hand it goes straight up into mid-air, like a rocket. Another turn and it makes a somersault like a tumbler pigeon, repeating it over and over. Then it wanders, seemingly with great labor, to the farthest limit of the arc, hesitates, considers, and then sweeps horizontally back with great speed.

Each New Year season there are contests in kite flying, the object being to cut the enemy's string and let his kite go. In preparation for this, a string is twisted of silk and coated with ground glass and porcelain mixed with glue. As it flies singing off the reel you feel toward such, much as a bird might feel toward a wall capped with broken bottles.

These contests are quite as exciting as anything seen on an American baseball field. The old men in thickly padded suits are seated on mats at some point where the view is unobstructed, while ordinary spectators fill the streets. The most tried and skillful man of the district has the kite in hand. One of the safeguards of the amusement is, that the actual combatants are many yards apart, sometimes nearly quarter of a mile, so there is no possible danger of a misunderstanding ending in a mêlée.

Little boys in red jackets and white pantaloons are everywhere on tiptoe of expectation for fallen string or stray kite.

One tournament in the capital we still remember vividly. Different wards of the city had entered the lists, and even the coolies were excited. After due ceremony the kites rose slowly from the chosen centres. They were far apart and seemed as little in danger of attacking each other as the extreme ends of the

Dipper. They drew apart until sufficient string was off the reel, and then gradually pulled together until the distance was spanned. Now they were face to face, nodding politely, schottishing back and forth, growing more animated till their motion assumed something of the form of a highland fling. Then they swooped at each other—passed and repassed—shot by at high speed—struck—one kite spun for a moment; then dived underneath—the spectators held their breath. Now strings were crossed and the fight began, each party letting off glue and glass filings as fast as his reel would spin. It was the calling out of reserves for the final charge—a moment later one kite remained riding triumphantly in the sky, while the other with tipsy motion floated off into the blue azure, the broken string falling over the roof-tops.

A little lad with radiant face and red coat caught the string and, in his haste, took a grip of it and ran toward home, forgetful of the glass filings and glue. Some one caught the other end and drew it through his hand. At once he dropped it and looked, and there a line oozed out of his chubby fingers as red as his New Year's jacket. His features suddenly reversed, and in bitterness and woe he went home to tell his mother of the sorrows and defeats of New Year's day. But over in the other ward there was feasting and music, and the mothers there said there never had been such kite-flying since the founding of the dynasty.

In the evening the Korean closes his doors to keep out Santa Claus, whom he calls Angwangi. Angwangi is an old man who lives in the upper air and collects material for New Year's gifts. As in other parts of the East, the Korean leaves his shoes at the door, and Angwangi comes down on New Year's eve and tries them on, leaving a memento of his visit. He is not the genial Santa Claus we know however, but a villainous old fiend, whose gifts consist of typhus fever, cholera, leprosy and the like. There is no joyful expectation, but the most dismal fear of Angwangi. When a child cries, just as the French mothers used to say "Malbroke or Marlborough is coming," so Korean mothers say "Hush or Angwangi will catch you." Yet as against other common evils of the Orient, the natives have a protection provided. One way is to bring all the shoes inside and keep a light burning for the night; but in certain cases bringing the shoes indoors exposes the inmates to other misfortunes, and so it has taken much thoughtful consideration and study to meet this case of Angwangi. After baiting him with this and that and attempting in vain to propitiate him, it was found that a common flour-sieve left at the door would attract his attention and render him oblivious to all the shoes of the capital, for he has a mania for counting the meshes of the sieve. He counts and counts, and before he is aware the night has fled, and his opportunity to scatter New Year's pestilence is gone. So a sieve is always left beside the shoe mat on New Year's eve.

As I mentioned in another chapter, stone fights are a characteristic of Korean New Year's season. Even young lads of ten and twelve will indulge in this, by way of practice for a real fight when they come of age. One day walking with a friend along the walls of the city near the West Gate, we came on some half-dozen boys throwing stones at a small group entrenched behind a mound on the other side of the wall. My friend who was emphatic in his manner attempted to remonstrate with the lads but they merely grinned at him and recommenced. We watched them to know what the end would be, finding much to interest us, until to our terror a stone grazed the wall of the city and struck the largest boy a tremendous blow in the mouth. My emphatic friend fairly shook him and said, "Didn't I tell you so?" The lad made no reply but as Bret Harte says:

> "He smiled a sort of sickly smile,
> And curled up on the floor,
> And the subsequent proceedings,
> Interested him no more."

Once when attempting an unexplored region through the south I was overtaken by this festive season, and yet it did not prove a time of unmixed happiness for me. The fact that no foreigner had been seen there before made me, to a miserable degree, the object of curiosity. The dogs in every town were simply beside themselves. They barked until overtaken by sheer exhaustion, when they lay down in despair, unable to do the occasion justice. An entire village, too, of the most immovable people on record, would collect, and have you pulled, handled, and inspected in the space of a few seconds. After a week of this, my Korean friend and I reached Tagu the capital of the southeastern province on the day preceding New Year's eve. The governor having heard that something was coming, sent a company of runners to intercept our entrance. We were made aware of their approach in the distance by their fluttering coats and red hat-streamers. The officer in charge carried a curved sabre, and gave his orders in a stentorian voice. He halted me and demanded my passport. After giving him this I was ordered to wait in a small room near the South Gate, till the governor should see the passport and decide what disposition should be made of me. Here I waited. Meanwhile the population of the district began to gravitate toward the small room, where soon every crevice and corner were filled with faces eager to see; and the struggle that went on among the sight-seers for points of vantage was very violent. The comments and opinions expressed were not complimentary. All delusions that I had labored under concerning my personal appearance left me that New Year's eve when I heard what those people had to say. "Look at the eyes! Green and upside down. Tremendous nose! Short coat and tight pantaloons. They must be out of cloth in his country. Behold the barbarian!" Happily the officer returned with a red card from the governor and an order to come at once. I have learned that in the Orient it is best to glide gently with the tide of ceremony, when no question of right or honor is involved. So I was shown in on horseback with two runners ahead, each carrying a paddle about as large as we see on a man-of-war's boats. These paddles are associated, not with the word *rōw*, but with the word *rŏw*, for they are used not to *pro*pel, but to *com*pel, being the wooden arms of the law to enforce order. When hurrying through the streets, I understood as never before the meaning of the scriptural phrase, "The sound of a great multitude," for the people who had collected for the past hour were after us pell-mell. We reached the quadrangle in front of the governor's *ya-*

men, and were told to wait. Here a confusion of dust and disorder commenced that is quite beyond description. Had I not been upon horseback, I should have been nipped like a ship among the icebergs; but the pony that had tried my patience for a week now stood friend for me, and made amends for past shortcomings. The only open space visible in all the square, was just behind the pony's heels, a yard or two in radius. The people climbed up on each other's backs, shouted, fought and struggled. The only consolation I had when I heard their question "Is he devil or man?" was a certain feeling of being associated with Tennyson's hero, "devil for ought they knew."

My Korean friend who had dismounted and who had had his white dress crumpled and his patience trampled underfoot, remarked to the people that they reminded him of a lot of cattle or swine, as far as their manners were concerned. His word was like a match to tinder, and we soon learned how great a matter a little fire kindleth. They resented this as one man, and were preparing to turn us out of town, when I left my pony and found shelter through a side gate in front of the *yamen*. Immediately on entering, the proprietor, who was a short man with a very red nose, showed true Oriental hospitality. A yard beyond his gate and he would have helped stone us, but the moment we entered he freely offered us the shelter and protection of his noisome den. It was an apartment rife with odors, cold and damp. The owner, however, felt not the cold, for his heart had been warmed by native *sul* (whiskey) and every word he spoke was charged with alcoholic atmospheres. He gave me his mat to sit upon, and while the front door filled with sight-seers, squeezed himself close up to my side and shouted at the top of his voice, How old was I, and where had I come from? While trying to satisfy his curiosity, word came that the governor was ready. Under an escort of men wearing the blue coats and red hat tassels, my Korean friend and I passed through gate and passageway up a dozen stone steps or so, and were before the governor, his retinue being ranged on each side of him. He asked a question or two—these I remember, Did we have a race of one-eyed cyclops in our country, or did we all wear two eyes? Was it true that Western people could pull their teeth out and replace them at will? After other ethnological and scientific inquiries the interview ended, and I was sent to the mayor of the city, being properly under his jurisdiction as to general behavior. With the same escort we passed through his gate, and found under the eaves of his office a row of prisoners seated on the ground wearing a *cangue*. A *cangue* belongs to the same family as stocks or ankle-squeezers, but is worn round the neck. It is a plank a foot or more in width, and some four feet long, with a hole through the middle. Opened by a hinge, it can be locked round the neck, and there you are with a collar, that for width and historical association surpasses that of Henry IV. of France or Queen Elizabeth herself. As we passed before this solemn row of prisoners, it looked like so many winking heads out drying on a row of boards such as you see Japanese women stretch cloth on; for only the head was visible, the rest of the person being concealed behind the collar. I began to feel oppressed by this judicial atmosphere that seemed to partake of the nature of anything in the world but New Year's eve. Various styles of collars we have worn with satisfaction, feeling that they fill an otherwise unhappy blank in the personal appearance; but the style of collar in vogue in that *yamen* compound, lacked the association of ladies and other respectable society.

The mayor of the city was specially cold in his reception. When I entered he was taken with a violent fit of coughing that lasted nearly all the interview. During one period of cessation he had a prisoner called, stretched on the ground before his window, and then beaten with the paddles I had seen carried through the streets. The beating was accompanied by pe-

THE CANGUE.

ACCORDING TO LAW.

culiar long-drawn notes to which the paddles kept time. The prisoner, meanwhile in agony, howled to the gods and spirits of his ancestors to witness that he was innocent. When the poor man had been reduced almost to a pulp, he confessed that he had done the deed, and was removed forthwith to have his wooden collar locked on again, and to spend the night under the droppings of the eaves. We departed without further ceremony, for we were aware of the unfriendly spirit behind such a reception. The escort had disappeared, and my Korean friend and I seemed quite alone. On passing out of the gate, a number of men caught Mr. Yi and tried to pull him back into the courtyard, where they threatened to decorate us with collar and full evening dress. By keeping between him and his pursuers, we made our escape to the little room where the short man lived, who had the very red nose and the inquiring disposition. Koreans are a slow people to move, but when they do become excited, especially if it is about nothing, they are very violent; and now I began to realize that my friend Yi's unguarded words, more especially his reference to swine, had brought a whirlwind upon us.

In the mob that pushed into the courtyard, I saw the form and cut of dress of the governor's chief secretary—each official grade has its particular uniform by which it can be recognized.

A word or two with him might avail something if I could only catch his ear. A moment later he came in through the press, and I had an opportunity to ask him if he would help me. "In what particular?" said he. "In this, it is our Western New Year's eve to-night, and I would like quiet that I may write a letter to my father and mother, for I always write them on New Year's eve." "Is your father alive?" asked the secretary with some surprise. "Yes," I said, "alive, and has a very high regard indeed for Korea." He at once told those nearest him that my father and mother were alive, and that I was going to write them about their Land of Morning Calm. Word passed that I was to be trusted, for I had been born of parents and showed unmistakable signs of filial affection. Gradually the tumult quieted, the people took their departure, and some of the old women ventured to the front door and shouted questions about my maternal ancestry. Neither years nor miles can carry one beyond the protection that the Orient recognizes in the sacred names, father and mother.

Mr. Yi looked as though a reprieve had come to him after sentence of death. He introduced himself to the chief secretary and told him it was quite a misunderstanding, that we had not come to declare war, but purely on an errand of peace. I had now liberty to write, and the secretary was much impressed at seeing me taking notes; for the ability to write is the *summum bonum* of a Korean gentleman's existence. He of course reasoned from this that I was not a barbarian, but a distinguished subject for entertainment, and so he provided an elaborate New Year's spread, and came with his friends to help enjoy it; while the governor, on the secretary's recommendation I know, added a present of dates and persimmons.

The short man with a very red nose had, as Koreans say, won face tremendously, for the refugees he sheltered had suddenly been elevated to the position of public guests. He became quite jubilant, while, if not the X-rays, the extraordinary rays that lit up his countenance beamed with more spirit than ever.

There is a Korean ceremony of watching out the Old Year; so to do us honor the company remained the greater part of the night, passing compliments, and asking questions about our customs and beliefs.

We left next day, and have not since seen the ancient city of Tagu, though memory still goes back to our New Year's visit. A company of sympathetic hermits saw us beyond the gates and, with due ceremony, expressed their farewells, "Go in peace!" and "In peace may we meet again!"

IX

THE KOREAN MIND

THE great problem that confronts all work in the Far East is the Oriental mind. It is comparatively easy to reach the heart, to gain the affection and esteem of the people, and yet at the same time to be perfectly mystified by the peculiar mental make-up that is the groundwork of all. So much of life seems reversed or standing on its head in their universe of thought, just as is actually the case in the universe of matter. The Korean says, If it is true that the world is round, then we in the West must have power, like flies, to walk on the ceiling of the under world; while we answer, No! it is you who are upside down. Thus are we born hopelessly reversed, and thus must we ever continue unless we are given the gift to be all things to all men—to stand on our heads too, and learn something of our brother Oriental eye to eye.

To this end we have to review many of our axioms of life, for we find them sadly upset in the East. With all due respect to Korea, one cannot but see that love has yielded up the ghost to what seems to be necessity. Unselfish love is a quantity foreign to the Oriental mind; in fact the Korean has no true word for love in his vocabulary; you have to arrive at the thought by a combination of terms. He talks of kindly condescension, reverence, esteem, etc., but he has no general word for love.

The husband marries a wife whom he does not love, and this is proper in the mind of the Orient; but on the death of the first he takes a second whom he does love, and this is all wrong, in fact is a sin, and he feels that he has indeed outraged his conscience. The wife was not meant to be loved, but simply as an inanimate object to serve her use in supporting one span of the family line from father to son. Planted deep in the mire, she stands bearing her portion of the weight of this ancestral bridge connecting the ages.

Once out walking, my wife and I found a man, like the ancient mariner, sitting alone on a stone weeping in a most hopeless way. What was the matter? He lifted his eyes for a moment and then bowed his head again and gave himself up to his grief. We persisted in knowing. His wife had left him he said, Aigo! Aigo! At last a true case of love it seemed. "But," we said, to try him with the philosophy of this world, "If she does not love you, why should you love her?" "Love! who loves her? But she made my clothes and cooked my food—how can I live without her? Aigo! Aigo!"

Neither does the independence of the West appeal to the Korean. The glory of the American Eagle with his *E pluribus unum*, he thinks to be sheer madness. Why men should ever think of such a horse-race existence, he cannot imagine. He conceives of life as a condition of subjection only. Independence to him suggests suspicion, mistrust of each other, lawlessness, etc. "Where are you going?" is the ordinary question of the street. "What's your business?" usually follows. "Whom is your letter from?" they demand—while all join in helping to read it. It would be an outrage not to share these commonplaces with every comer. So we find them doubling up over work that is mere child's play; bearing the inconvenience of companions in places where they might be doubly comfortable alone, were it not for their dread of independence, which seems to run contrary to the flow of all their mental faculties.

In education too, we are at the antipodes. We aim at the development and preparation of the student in a practical way for life before him; the Korean has no such thought. He aims to fix or asphyxiate the mind, in order that he may shut the present out and live only in the past. Development is our idea; limitation his. A Western student rejoices in a variety of attainments and the number of branches in which he has been introduced; while the Korean, in the fact that he knows nothing of any subject but the reading and writing of Chinese characters. Twenty years of seclusion in order that he may be able to read and write; and many a student fails even of this after so long a time. With us education is an exercise of the faculties, in order that the mind may grow; in Korea it is like a foot bandage or plaster of paris jacket for the mind: once fairly put on, and all growth and development is at an end. Hence the fact, Confucian scholars more than any others oppose the preaching of Christianity.

However shiftless an American may be, he feels deep down in his heart that labor is ennobling. In theory, at any rate, children are taught the dignity of labor. In Korea there exists the very opposite idea. The word for labor is *il*, and its secondary meanings are damage, loss, evil, misfortune, all of which ideas are associated with, and expressed by, the word. An idle existence brings with it no stings of conscience, in fact the native who can scheme to do nothing, proves by all the logic of antiquity his right to unquestioned nobility.

To us the mind acts as a sort of telegraphic communication between the heart and the countenance. The joy or sorrow that overtakes us, is flashed from one to the other, so that we learn naturally to read the inner soul by these waves of light and shadow. In Korea the mind has other duties, the principal one of which is to cut off communication between these two, and to make them entirely independent; to flood the countenance with mere surface expression, or, if need be, to transform it into an expressionless wilderness. A Korean, in his phlegmatic way, shows utter indifference when his wife or his father dies; while a Westerner, true to his feelings, expresses by voice and countenance all that his heart experiences. It needs but a short sojourn in the East to teach us that heart and countenance are not necessarily in communication; that there are beneath, hidden depths and undercurrents never dreamed of.

One is often pained by mistaking mere appearance for reality. Truth is not loved for truth's sake, but only in so far as it is necessary for appearances. The mind seems incapable of understanding what some of the commonest phases of truth are. When the Emperor goes out on procession the whole city is ransacked to contribute to the show. Red earth is sprinkled to keep the sacred palanquin from passing over polluted soil, but the sprinkling is less than the salt and pepper in an Irish stew.

There is great pretense at bustle. Soldiers in confused haste are fleeing everywhere. Even the ponies take part and bite viciously. Feathers and flags; straggling lines of natives in uniform of five hundred years ago; squads with rattling poles to provide the necessary music; kettle drums, sometimes beaten, and sometimes merely threatened; thousands of pairs of baggy trousers and straw shoes; red coats and peacock feathers; magnificent officials, perched on high saddles, holding on with both hands, bumping up and down, ready at any moment to fall backward or headlong; imposing banners with Chinese characters; pipes to smoke and pipes to blow; Remington rifles and matchlock guns; bows and arrows and incense bottles; Chicago corned beef and charms against devils; bear's gall and snake skin; modern helmets and ancient hats; confusion, disorder, magnificence; grandeur and squalor; ten thousand strong, moving, rolling, bundling, in dust and cloud and clatter, a screaming mass of discord and color. The Westerner is amazed, while the native is in an ecstasy of delight at so magnificent an ensemble, with no thought of how becoming, or genuine, or useful, the component parts may be.

The more hangers-on he has the greater the man. A servant knows of no better way to honor his master in the eyes of the community, than to urge him to hire an extra coolie or two to loaf about his kitchen or squeeze cash from those who call. The house may be falling into ruins, gates and doors off the hinges, poverty staring in at every chink, and yet, if only sufficient ceremony and commotion is kept up, the owner's position as a man of importance is assured; appearance, not reality, being the aim of life.

It is a saying in the West that when you cannot depend upon a man's word, all hope of him as a moral quantity is gone. To apply such a rule to the East would be to condemn an entire continent. The Korean cannot understand why we should arbitrarily lay so much stress upon a man's word. Words they consider to be the cheapest ingredient of life. To demand that they be held sacred is to attempt to build righteousness out of what costs us nothing, and to interfere materially with the even flow of conversation—a much more important consideration than the words themselves. And so their intercourse proceeds upon the understanding that words may mean nothing more than a passing compliment, as we say, How do you do? and are answered by, How do you do? neither one, for a moment, taking it as a question to be answered by an explicit statement.

When a lady in the West sends word to an unwelcome caller that she is out, there follows an unpleasant controversy between reason and conscience; but when a Korean says that he is out or is ill, he returns to his cushions in the feeling that he is indeed gentlemanly in thus saying the proper thing. When I first reached Korea, I endeavored to be faithful to my friends, and to be on hand when they called. One of the most common parting salutations was, "Nail do orita" (I will come again to-morrow). Many never came; those who did left with the same promise, so that sooner or later I found that all my best friends failed to keep their word. After a while it dawned upon me that words and promises did not necessarily mean what they expressed, and here I found I was on safe ground, able to walk in a measure peacefully and trustfully with my Oriental friend.

So we remain at the antipodes of thought. It will take much mental exploration and engineering to bring us within hailing distance of each other; but we trust still that the day is coming when our hearts may be united and our minds may, in a measure at least, be agreed.

X

THE KOREAN GENTLEMAN

The calm and composure that environs a Korean gentleman is one of the mysteries of the Orient. Embarrassed he may be by a thousand debts, and threatened by a hungry wolf through every chink in his mud cabin, yet the placidity of his life continues unruffled. He is a master of a composure that forms the groundwork of other characteristics. From Confucius he has learned to mortify every natural impulse, and to move as though he acted his part on a stage where a single misdirected smile or thoughtless measure would upset the greatest piece on record. His choicest word is *yei*, meaning proper form. If he only keeps *yei*, he may offend against every command in the decalogue and still be a superior man, in fact may be perfectly holy. If he breaks *yei*, he is covered with confusion, and counts himself the vilest of the vile.

Yei of course is Confucianism. If you speak a word in disparagement of *yei*, the gentleman is frantic, forgets *yei* altogether for the moment in his effort at violence.

The Korean speaks respectfully of Mencius

as *Măng*, and of Confucius as *Kong*, so that the names coupled together would read *Măng-kong*.

This word *măng-kong* has unfortunately another meaning, namely, the croaking of frogs. A Korean gentleman, who had travelled much abroad, and had learned foreign languages, came home quite outdone with Korea's ancient civilization, and particularly set against Confucianism. In one of his public lectures in Seoul to a company of Koreans, he made use of the word *măng-kong*. "What benefit," said he, "has Confucius been to Korea? Those best versed in his doctrines are the most helpless and useless people we have. They simply sit and croak *măng-kong, măng-kong* to everything." A scholar who heard him, and whom I know well, left the meeting in a piping fury. "Nothing," said he, "but the knife for men like that." He had forgotten *yei* for the moment, and was willing to be an assassin, if only he might defend its sacred name.

Anything that interferes with the rigid fulfillment of *yei* is of course to be avoided, for which reason no gentleman indulges in manual labor, or in fact in labor of any kind. His life consists in one supreme command of coolie service, while the coolie responds to every order. The lighting of his pipe or the rubbing of ink on the inkstone, must be done for him. Down to the simplest requirement of life he does nothing, so his hands become soft and his finger nails grow long. From constant sitting his bones seem to disintegrate and he becomes almost a mollusk before he passes middle life.

When once they have attained to this physical condition of pulp, they are in a measure immune from the thumps and shocks of ordinary life. It was my misfortune once to ride through a rough and mountainous country in company with a Korean gentleman. By keeping a constant hold on the halter rope, I managed to escape a back somersault whenever the pony jumped. I warned Mr. Cho of the danger he ran in sitting bolt upright on the pack, without girders or supports of any kind to protect him. He remarked, in reply, that it was not good Korean custom to hold on the halter as I advised, and so we proceeded. When the sun grew hot, he added to his already top-heavy condition by opening an umbrella. The startled pony with one bound, shot Mr. Cho backward out of the saddle, and his fall, which is the point of my story, was marvellous to behold. On the uneven surface of the road he flattened out like a ball of paris plaster. Jacket and pantaloons were lost sight of, even the hat, like a spot on the sun, was but an irregularity of color on an otherwise flattened surface. But from this mass came forth the man, illustrating how we have all proceeded from original protoplasm, for he pulled himself together, and said he was none the worse, though I should certainly have been damaged seriously by such a fall.

Not all the gentry by any means are scholars, though they ought to be if they came up to the standard of Confucian requirement. Those who have attained to this are marked and honored men; they are all but worshipped by the mass of the people, and are given the freedom of every city in the Kingdom; they are admitted as distinguished guests into the presence of the highest, free of pass. Chinese characters seem to have for these few a consuming fascination. Not so much the thought conveyed as the character itself, seems the object of veneration. From them he "builds" (*chita*) forms of expression and verses as a child builds enchanted castles from blocks of different sizes; and as there is no limit to the variations and combinations possible, so there is no limit to the charm they possess. Two scholars can find sufficient to interest them for a day in a single character, and as there are in use some 20,000 characters, they have a fund of interest to draw on that will last for half a century. No attempt is ever made to write more than original ditties or mottoes; anything approaching to an original work in Chinese would be like an attempt to outdo Homer in Greek—presumption unheard of. So the scholar plays his life away with this unending rosary of ideographs, that entwine not only his neck, but his mind, and heart, and soul.

For the unlettered gentry Chinese has no charm. They keep a few learned expressions at their finger ends, as a sort of bulwark of defence when hard pressed, but as far as possible they avoid the subject. Their life, since shut off from intellectual pleasure, consists of material pleasure, dress and enjoyment. This class of scholar is exceedingly common in Korea. In immaculate white he emerges from the holes and corners of every mud village. If he is an official of importance, he does not walk alone, but is assisted by the arms on each side. If he ventures by himself, it is with a magnificent stride that clears the street of indifferent passers, and commands only on-lookers. In one hand is a pipe three feet long, in the other a fan; over his eyes two immense discs of dark crystal, not to assist him in seeing, but to insure his being seen. How precious these are! Many a man will forego the necessaries of life if only he can gain a pair of *Kyüng-ju*, (spectacles), and so cover himself with glory before an on-looking assemblage. I once offended greatly against *yei* in an effort to befriend an impecunious gentleman, who had told me of his financial embarrassments. He was at the time wearing a pair of dark crystals, and thinking to make him a present under cover of a purchase, I offered him thirty *yang* or six American dollars for his glasses. He was amazed to think that I should virtually ask them for nothing, for he had paid equal to fifteen dollars for them and a bargain they had been at that. This is one of the absurdities of the Orient, where a man pays two or three months' income for something absolutely worthless. Oriental methods are so extremely absurd that there is no hope of an Occidental demonstration by which to rectify them.

The impecuniosity of a Korean gentleman is also a profound mystery. I have figured for years on the question as to how an idle man, with nothing left to-day, shall outlive to-morrow; but he lives, dresses just as well and misses none of his meals. He will tell you frankly that the last of his hopes for a livelihood have perished, he is financially a total wreck, and his present condition is one of clinging to the rocks, where he is in momentary peril of the devouring element. You are exercised deeply on his behalf; much more deeply, you learn later, than he himself is. Months pass and he is still in the same condition—a condition *in extremis*, no better, no worse. By way of encouragement I have said: "You have managed to eat and live for a month and more on nothing, just continue on in the same manner and you will do very well." "Eat and live," says he, "of course every dog eats and lives; you would not expect me to lie down and die, would you?" And he leaves in disgust, feeling that the delicate points of an Oriental question can never penetrate the shell that encases the barbarian's brain.

The fact that tradesmen and business people are regarded as low, encourages the Korean gentleman to neglect thought and training in this line. He is a veritable child in business. Many a foreigner entrusts his affairs to his native teacher, and wonders why they should turn out so unsatisfactorily in the hands of a native. If business must be transacted an honest "boy" will quite outdo in executive skill the best and most honest scholar.

Not only in business but in other affairs of life the Korean gentleman is a master of inaccuracy. He pretends to be absolutely certain of everything under the sun, and no subject ever daunts him or is beyond his ability to elucidate. The slightest clue gives him a key to the whole; merely let him see the smoke from the funnel and he will explain to you the why and wherefore of a steam engine. He will tell you what a comet's tail is composed of, or what color the dog is that causes the eclipse of the moon. He compares the minor details of life about him with what went on in the days of king *Sun*—a contemporary of Noah—with as much assurance as we would talk of the events of yesterday. The new arrival in the Land of Morning Calm begins to think what a marvel of information this man is, and what a fund of accurate knowledge he has acquired, and he a heathen, too. It is only when you put his statements to the test you find he is astray in everything. By the rarest accident he may be right, but it is the exception. He has no intention of deceiving you. The defect lies in the fact that there is something radically wrong with his manner of reasoning, and of putting two and two together.

He has a profound contempt for woman, speaking of her generally as *kechip* or female. He takes for wife the one his father bargains for, raising no question as to her looks, health or avoirdupois. She is a subject altogether beneath the consideration of a member of the male sex with its massive understanding. She is relegated to the inner enclosure and lives a secluded life. He refers to her as *kösiki* (what-you-may-call-her), or *keu* (she), and never loses an opportunity of showing how little is the place she occupies in his extensive operations. If the truth were told, however, we would know that the little woman within that enclosure is by no means the cypher he pretends her to be; but that she is really mate and skipper of the entire institution, and that no man was ever more thoroughly under petticoat government than this same Korean gentleman.

His prime object in life is to have a son who will sacrifice to his shades when he is dead and gone. The boy is expected to obey his father implicitly. If he but develop that trait, he may grow up to be quite as useless or more so than his sire, and yet be a model son. If no son is born to him, he adopts a nephew or near relative as the best substitute under the circumstances. But the stranger never wholly takes the place of the real son, who is regarded in this life as his strong right arm, and in the life to come as his eternal satisfaction.

In order to make sure of this eternal life through posterity, the gentleman marries his son off when he is still a mere boy, sometimes but nine or ten years of age. Child marriage is one of the old and respected customs in Korea. That it is not more common is because it requires an outlay of money which parents are not always willing or able to make, and so the lad is sometimes left unmarried till he can provide for himself.

The serious question in the life of a Korean gentleman is the service of his ancestor-shades.

THE WARDROBE OF THE GENTRY.

KOSIKI (WHAT-YOU-MAY-CALL-HER)

His life is marked by periods of mourning—three years for parents, and lesser periods for more distant relatives. A succession of fasts and feasts, requiring forms of dress and outlays of money, consumes more of his time and means than all the provision for the family living. To neglect these forms would degrade him to the level of a Mohammedan who had renounced his faith.

We have glimpses occasionally of the gentleman's ability, as he shares in the games of the outer guest chamber. Chess and *patok*, a kind of draughts, he plays frequently. A half hour's teaching will show him the moves on a foreign chess board, and a very respectable player he becomes from the outset. His best work is seen in the leisurely development of the game. Rapidity or excitement upsets him. I have seen excellent players, master amateurs of the board, who have had no gift whatever for the solving of problems. When one attempt failed they would give it up and say " It can't be done." This again proves the jelly-fish in his nature, his condition being passive, not active. Anything like a determined effort he is entirely incapable of, as the mollusk is incapable of performing the feats of the shark or sword-fish. Were I to choose one common saying from the language that enters more largely into the life and character of the Korean gentleman than any other, it would be *Mot hao* or *Hal su upso* (No help for it or It can't be done).

A marked characteristic of a Korean gentleman's home is its entire respectability. There is frankness and freedom in speech, but no looseness; and few conditions exist that would offend in the best ordered Western household. Strange to say, even in a home where there are a number of concubines, propriety and good order obtain. I once made a journey to Japan with a strict and devout Korean Confucianist, Mr. Cheung. He had heard much of Christ and Christianity, and while he assented to, and rejoiced in, whatever of it agreed with his ancient faith, he remained a Confucianist firm as ever. We took ship in one of the ports of Korea and started for Japan. He had heard of the adoption of Western life and customs in the Sunrise Kingdom, and was desirous to see something of the benefits it would confer upon a race. The first thing he saw was the depravity of the women; "Selling themselves," said he, "before the eyes of onlookers, and for copper money too." A year's residence in the country confirmed him in the belief that what he had seen was not the exception, but a national trait. "When women are so depraved the men must be equally so. They know nothing of Confucius and no fear of God is before their eyes. Western civilization merely tends to make their depravity more exceedingly depraved." He lived as in a kind of nightmare—horror-stricken by nudity and obscenity such as he had never dreamed of in his isolated kingdom. He saw two drunken English and American sailors, and the so-called respectables whose life was but a whirl of pleasure seeking. "Your Christ," said he, "has but a meagre hold upon you after all." He had put off his dress and laid aside his topknot, but his heart remained still faithful to the garments of his ancient faith. The more he saw of life abroad, the more he sighed for his straw roof and mud hut, where modesty and virtue had honor still, and where life was lived with some degree of regard for the teachings of the ancient sages.

So he passes from us one of the last and most unique remains of a civilization that has lived its day. His composure, his mastery of self, his moderation, his kindliness, his scholarly attainments, his dignity, his absolute good-for-nothingness, or better, unfitness for the world he lives in—all combine to make him a mystery of humanity, that you cannot but feel kindly toward and intensely interested in.

XI

KOREA'S PRESENT CONDITION

THIS small peninsula presents to those interested in missions perhaps the most startling field opened up during this missionary century. Till within the last decade it was closed and barred against every one. Even the Chinese, who, up till 1894, received the yearly ambassador with Korea's tribute, knew as little as others of the inner life of the people. Since the distant past, Korea has remained entirely alone, and has endeavored to work her way independent of others. The result has been that she has built up, as suitable for her life as a hermit, systems that have been subjected to violent agitations since she has entered the company of treaty-making nations.

At no point in her history of a thousand years has there been such overwhelming force brought to bear upon her cherished customs, as at the present time. A war with Japan three hundred years ago, cost Korea a great deal of life, and almost her individuality, destroyed her ancient monuments, and robbed her of her arts and manufactures; but when the enemy withdrew, she revived slightly and continued to exist. A hundred years later, a Manchurian swoop upon the capital left her in nominal subjection only; and she still remained mistress of her own fortunes. But the opening of the ports has rung a knell to ancient Chosön (Korea). The influence that enters through these gates is an enemy that knows of no retreat, so that Korea's continuance as a hermit is no longer possible.

The present period threatens to destroy not only her established means of livelihood, but also her social systems; and unless Christianity be brought her, nothing but superstition, agnosticism, and chaos will be her portion.

Her entrance into foreign life has been through a hideous nightmare, beginning with the Tonghaks, continuing through the Japan-China war, and closing with the murder of the Queen. No wonder the Queen questioned the success of international fraternities. It is generally admitted that the rising of the Tonghaks was instigated by outside parties, who desired to bring on a war with China. Korea had no desire for independence. She regarded China as a child regards a parent—one from whom it would be unnatural to sever relationship, especially since this parent had been indulgent enough to leave her free to carve out her own fortunes. She felt in fact honored by recognition from the great middle kingdom, which is the glorious centre of a Korean's universe. The battle cry of "Freedom for Korea!" was one of those pretty conceits or deceits of the Orient, meant simply to throw unwary Occidentals off the scent. Such a cry reminds one of the fox, who being anxious lest the mother hen should sit too hard upon her chickens, made a special raid upon the poultry yard to rescue them from their thralldom.

The great burden of the war fell on North Korea. P'yöng-yang was devastated. The country for miles about became a wilderness, poisoned by the stench from the battlefield. At last the armies crossed the Yalu, and the nation settled down under a new regime dictated by Japan. But a certain Stonewall Jackson stood in the way of Japan's reforms. The ablest minister they could send found himself outwitted, checkmated, defeated, until he beat a retreat, gave up the fight, and went home. Who could but admire the courage, the shrewdness, the womanliness of this little Queen of Korea, who standing for the best interests of her country, so ably outgeneralled the Japanese minister and his wisest aides! Who would have believed that so foul a deed could be committed in an age of fair play! Four hundred men, pretending to stand for civilization, dressed in western uniforms with stars, gold lace and epaulettes, speaking the most graceful language of the Orient, made their way over the palace-wall at night, their mission being to murder one helpless woman, and she the Queen of Korea. One is amazed to think that among four hundred men there was not a single manly heart, but all four hundred of them unspeakable cowards, from the officer in command to the craven coolie in the rear. The common story, without question the true one, is: They hacked the Queen to death with "gallant" *samauri* swords, poured kerosene on her body and burned it to prevent recognition. They killed three or four other palace women to make sure they had the right one, and then marched out—noble four hundred! The people of Korea were horror-stricken, while the King himself remained a prisoner from October, 1895, to February, 1896. Then he made his escape into the Russian Legation, and the world that was civilized and aware of the facts shouted, hurrah!

But to enter more closely upon the facts. The year 1894 was one of special darkness for Chosön. With the opening of the first moon there were rumors of Tonghaks everywhere, and not a native called but had some dire tale of massacre to tell. The Tonghaks were God-worshippers and man-slayers. They ate spirit medicines, and could kill by a look. They said a rifle bullet would have no more effect on them than Burns' whittle on Hornie. We were all full of

Tonghak. The government seemed to have been struck by leprosy or some other ghastly paralysis. Officials were plundered, the authority of His Majesty was trampled under foot, and so with outstretched hand, he implored Tă-guk (the Great Empire of China) to help him. Tă-guk came in with a lot of ragamuffins, and the Tonghaks increased as the season advanced. Friend Yi, who had shared my joys and sorrows for six years, went in command of a company to help the sublime generalissimo of China annihilate the Tonghaks. Yi refuses to tell the experiences that befell him during this march southward. He came back neither in disgrace nor condemned to be beheaded, and so I conclude that he is one of the most unsuccessful military officers in the Far East. Meanwhile China had stirred up so much trouble, that Japan came in to put it down and they two declared war.

At that time I was building a house on the east coast at Wönsan or Gensan, and had in my employ some twenty Chinamen. They were confident that a couple of months would suffice Tă-guk to change the Sunrise Kingdom into a region of everlasting darkness, and that the few remaining *wo-jen* would perish. On July 25th, the *wo-jen* sunk the *Kowshing* with 1,200 Chinamen on board. They sighted the vessel and overhauled her with the *Naniwa kan*.

The transport ship was as helpless as Honolulu would be in case of an attack by sea, and so she dropped anchor. A Japanese official went on board and ordered the Chinese to follow as prisoners of war. Why the Chinese did not shoot the officer I do not know. They refused to go to Japan, and when the English captain threatened to leave the ship, they said they would shoot him if he did. So the *Naniwa* cleared her decks and prepared for action. One tremendous explosion, and the *Kowshing* like the *Maine* was deep under water with her helpless cargo, generals and privates struggling for their lives. It is said upon good authority that Japan turned her machine guns on these poor wretches. Can it possibly be true that Japan is as vindictively savage as some of these acts during the late war have shown her to be! The sinking of the *Kowshing*, the massacre at Port Arthur, the murder of the Queen of Korea! We wish Japan well, but one need not be a military officer or a diplomat to know that no wishing can avail to bring permanent success out of such barbarism.

From amongst those struggling in the water the Japanese picked up the English officers, brought them aboard the *Naniwa*, rubbed the captain dry lest he should take cold, warmed him with champagne, and we were told, presented him with three thousand dollars which he might return on the day of judgment. A multitude of bubbles from the pattering of the leaden hail and the drowning Chinamen—and the sea was calm and beautiful. Four days later Japan turned her trained Western forces on a scattered rabble at Asan. The fleeing Chinamen made a circuit of Kang-wön, Whanghă and P'yöng-an provinces to P'yöng-yang. Along the way they spread terror everywhere. Korean women escaped to the hills and old men sat down and cried as these vandals from the Empire of Heaven plundered and robbed. Certainly the passage of the two armies contrasted greatly, and if Japan ever scored in Korea, it was when she led her soldiers through the Peninsula, paying as they went, and respecting the lives and property of the people. Into P'yöng-yang the Chinese bundled, there joining the forces of General Tso, helping to devour the two hundred pigs that a Korean told me were slaughtered daily for the army.

Meanwhile troops had landed at Wönsan. One bright Sunday morning in August as we were assembled in a Christian meeting, a half-dozen transports were sighted on the horizon. The hills everywhere were lined with eager and expectant natives, watching these fire ships and wondering what death-dealing cargo they would bring. It was not noon till the hills

WONSAN, JAPANESE SETTLEMENT.

WONSAN, CHINESE SETTLEMENT.

that had known only a people dressed in white were alive with diminutive soldiers, uniformed in blue, knapsacked and rifled. My twenty-three Chinamen had lost hope in the god of war. The old cook trembling in mortal terror, came rubbing his hands, bowing to my wife and crying: "Save me! Oh! save me!" She saved him by stowing him in an inner room behind the bed; a leg of chicken and a piece of pie were given him, and the Chinaman forgot the horrors of war under these reviving conditions of peace. Japs were everywhere. My friend Yi went out to talk with some of them, and they confessed that they were ready for England as well as China, if she liked to take a hand. A sage once said, "A big man for peace, a little man for conceit, and a woman for war." The Japanese are noted for their women and their little men—in fact they are the littlest men on record.

Two days later the army moved out of the port toward Seoul, one hundred and eighty-five miles distant. Then came a month when Wönsan was left unprotected, at the mercy of the Chinese, who could, at a moment's notice, have murdered the entire community. My house builders had fled, and bricks, mortar and timbers were lying in confusion. Reports reached us every day that the enemy was right on us, death was frequently in our ears. It was a time of earnestness, for at the hands of these savages from Kirin, wife and family would have received no mercy. The available firearms were looked to; the cook, boy and other natives said, "Master, if a fight comes we are with you." Though powerless, this desire to be faithful was gratifying. Later a Russian ship came by and some of the missionaries left; but my wife refused unless the husband went too. This was impossible, as the hope of the terrified natives rested on the Christian teacher's remaining. Great was the anxiety as the days passed, and the Chinese outposts and scouts came down to the very port to spy on us. One heavy summer night we sat together listening in the open veranda. Was it to be the tramp of soldiers overland or search-lights by sea? That morning an explosion had been heard. A ball of fire was seen coming from the north, moving toward the centre of the harbor, and there it exploded. We had heard the report which the natives regarded with fear. As we sat looking out seaward, one faint light was seen toward Port-Lazareff. It was stationary and I guessed that a native fisherman had lighted it. There it rested for a half-hour or more, then it seemed to gather motion, and to turn southeast toward the usual anchorage of the Chinese fleet. On it came till we discovered by its rapid motion, that a ship was in port. Had a Chinese man-of-war eluded the guards and were we between the fires, or was it a Japanese? The lights in the port-town were extinguished, and every heart waited. It was a Japanese transport with one thousand soldiers on board. We were grateful, and I take pleasure in recording here that we felt safe in the hands of the Japanese. They were less given to drunkenness and disorder than Western soldiers, and in nine cases out of ten acted as an enlightened nation; but in the tenth and test case they showed the old spots of the leopard with the varnish off.

Some ten thousand troops in all arrived in rapid succession by transport, and moved west toward P'yŏng-yang. A few days later the city had fallen, and dead Chinamen marked the course of the retreating army.

The medical corps put the wounded Chinese through Western forms of treatment, and redcross members were evident, apparently on missions of mercy. These acts were so widely heralded and so skillfully published in the Western world, that some were inclined to question the genuineness of the sympathy expressed. But Japan deserves credit for having surgeons and nurses abundant and skillful, showing her power to adapt herself to Western ways even in the storm and stress of war.

The skill with which the Japanese managed their commissariat and kept in touch with the source of supply, showed them indeed a very wonderful people. Their bridges they carried, their fuel, rice, beef and soy. No soldiers could have been better equipped, even to luxuries. The remainder of the campaign was one round of victory in Manchuria, at the mouth of the Yalu, at Port Arthur, and later, before Wei-hai-wei. I asked an English captain how they conducted themselves at the battle of the Yalu. "Their manœuvring was splendid," said he, " apparently no better seamen afloat." Startling indeed was this combination of big guns and little men.

For weakness and puerile imbecility, commend all the world to China. Brave Admiral Ting, who fought his best, had to commit suicide to prevent the disgrace of being beheaded at Peking. Captain Choy in command of the torpedo boats, was also on the condemned list. It has been said that there are no lunatic asylums in the Far East; but a glimpse at the government in Peking must convince every one, that for an assemblage of incapables they are very remarkable indeed.

Korea was now firmly in the grasp of Japan. The King was obliged to proclaim his independence. That he had no desire to do so, is evident from the very civilization that he and all other kings of Korea prize so highly. China to him was "Tă-guk" or "Chun-guk," the Great or Middle Kingdom; while Japan was Wai-guk, the despised land of dwarfs. Then came reforms so called. Off with the wide sleeves, and away with the long pipes. They were ordered to wear black. Korea has no black dye and so the black to be worn was to come from Japan, all of which greatly offended the natives, and made them hate the Japanese more than ever. It shows again Japan's insufficiency for the task on her hands. This seesawing continued from March till October, 1896. The Queen, whom all admit to have been a stronger character than the King, opposed these mock reforms vigorously, determined that her country should not come under the dominion of Japan. The fact too that Japanese influence put into office outlaws, whom the King had sentenced to death years before, showed the real attitude of Japan toward her weaker neighbor. She compelled the King to pardon Söh Kwang Pom and others. The absurdity of putting those the King hated and feared into his very presence as office-bearers, can only be explained on the ground of the absurdity of the Oriental mind. However capable a sojourn abroad may have made these exiles, it was most impolitic, not to say brutal, for Japan to coerce Korea into reform through their hands. The morale of the move was entirely out of joint.

The year labored on till October 8th, 1895, when in the early morning we were awakened by sounds of firing in the direction of the palace. Three of us walked over to see what was the matter. The side gate was open and many natives in dishevelled confusion were passing out. Two companies of Japanese soldiers were also seen coming from the interior. We were told that Hong, general of the Korean army, had been shot where we stood, a half hour before. We were ignorant of the meaning of this *coup d' etat*. The Japanese were evidently in full possession of the palace. Later in the day a rumor was circulated that the Queen had been murdered. Mr. Geo. Heber Jones and I were invited to remain near the apartments of the King, with Generals Dye and Legendre, and to assist as we could in interpreting the tragic mystery. The plight into which His Majesty had fallen was pitiful to behold. He wept for his Queen, the Japanese he said had murdered her. Could no one help him in this time of need! He would cut off his hair and weave shoes of it for those who would avenge her death. But the palace was close guarded; Japanese soldiers were quartered at the gate; Korean traitors held the King a prisoner. Nothing but a strong force and a declaration of war could have rescued him. Russia, England and America could only call daily and express such sympathy as was possible. Evidently the King's older brother—if not his father—was a traitor too. The murderers were arrested and taken to Japan. They were tried and acquitted, and this again made the King feel more than ever that his deadly enemies were the *wai-in* or *wo-jen*. Though the government at Tokyo washed its hands of the affair, it did not hesitate to take advantage for its own profit of what these cutthroats had done. This also had its damaging influence, not only on the Korean mind, but on the minds of others as well. Not even a hill god or a kitchen joss could acknowledge such dealings as honest.

Meanwhile the royal prisoner and crown prince eked out their cheerless existence. There seemed indeed no hope of escape. A few women's chairs went daily through the gates, but there was no exit for royalty.

A certain fiasco occurred during this time in which American missionaries were involved. They were criticised for having opinions regarding the death of the Queen and the King's present condition; it was claimed that they were interfering in politics. The question however was not one of politics, but of common mercy.

The year 1896 opened unauspiciously for His

Majesty still a prisoner of those whom he hated. There was a quiet plot working its underground way, and a loyal heart or two were bent on his rescue. Mr. Yi Pöm Chin, a relative whose ancestral seat is the royal house of Chön-ju, was in communication. He had stood by the King in other days when there was danger. He had taken the Dowager Queen Cho, Queen Min and the crown prince and princess to his country home during the émeute of 1884, and kept them till the King was restored. His father led the way against the Americans at Kangwha years ago, and he himself carries a bullet mark in his left arm, and suffers the pains of a broken ankle for his loyalty in days gone by. He was passing by stealth, closely written messages that reached the King through the hands of the *nai-in* or palace maids. They came and went inspected by the guards as they passed the gates. The cold days of February prompted Mr. Yi to regale the shivering guards on hot dishes of various kinds. They were feasted frequently, never suspecting the meaning of it. On the 11th of February the King stowed his slight person into the back of a woman's chair, and a palace maid named Pak sat before him. The crown prince was likewise tucked in, and slowly they started for the gateway. The guards having been feasted that cold morning were inclined to be good to everybody. They gave only a hurried glance at the chair, and Miss Pak said, "Please put down the front, why should you lift it so cold a morning?" "Pass on," said the guard, and the second chair followed likewise. On they moved to the foreign part of the city, and an hour later the world read the telegram, "The King of Korea has escaped from the palace and is in the Russian legation." Mr. Yi Pöm Chin who had engineered his escape was made chief minister, and the labor and sorrow and effort of Japan vanished into smoke.

The war passed like a cyclone over North Korea, leaving the country despoiled of its population, its ancestral groves and tablets. Confucianism binds a man to one piece of ground, separate him from that particular place and you have separated him from his gods; so the population that came back after the war, came back to a certain degree without their deities and shrines. Mr. Moffett, a missionary of well-deserved fame, was on the ground, with a knowledge of the language and a burning desire to have the people see Christ as Saviour, and the result has been that multitudes have come and a great revival has spread over the land. We trust that through much of the North the idols are gone never to be replaced.

We believe that now is a special time to bring the gospel to these people, for remarkable changes are taking place in their material world. It is well known to every one acquainted with Korea that the ordinary native dress is white cotton. It is the most extravagant and, withal, useless garb that one could imagine for a land subject to extremes of temperature, as this peninsula is; but it is a dress that carries in every fold ancestral associations, and has come to be thought the most dignified and becoming outfit in the world. Cotton therefore is in demand in Korea, as woolen goods are at home, and the weaving of this is the most important calling in Korea, giving employment to a large percentage of the people. The ports are opened, and in come bales of foreign cotton, cheaper than the natives can manufacture; native weaving is compelled to give way, as purchasers North and South find it more to their taste and pocket to dress in Western goods.

Work in metal is on the decrease as well, quantities being shipped in from Japan for the manufacture of pipes—articles as common here as teaspoons are at home. Castor beans that were grown to supply oil for lamps have disappeared, and a cheap kind of kerosene from Philadelphia does the lighting for Korea. The use of empty kerosene cans has all but annihilated the water bucket and crock-maker's trades. Dyestuffs are being crowded out by the introduction of cheaper and more attractive qualities from Japan. Axes, knives, nails and in fact all kinds of hardware are imported and sold cheaper than the native manufacture. Telegraph lines to the four points of the peninsula, while appreciated and prized by the foreigner, are hated by the native broker and travelling merchant, whose profits have been cut off by this constant communication with the capital. Money has become more and more valueless. Rice has gone up to five times its cash value since the opening of the ports, and most of the articles in daily use have quadrupled in the same time.

For this reason the native ships his beans and fish away in autumn, in order to raise money, thus endangering the lives of those depending on him during the long winter to follow.

In this destruction of the native's means of livelihood, no new calling seems to have arisen by which he can help to clothe and feed his people. Nothing has been provided to fill up the vacancy, and so the land is swarming with idlers and petty merchants, who make a doubtful living in handling foreign goods. The poverty of Korea is extreme; the manner of life and habits of the people such as to confirm one in the belief that they have reached the lowest condition possible; and so we look for a financial change, which must of necessity be for the better.

There can be no doubt that the resources of the country are great, but as they remain undeveloped they afford no amelioration of existing conditions.

While China has continued in the main uninfluenced by Western life, because of her industrial prosperity, Korea's financially helpless condition tells how powerfully she is to be influenced by intercourse with other nations. The average Korean is as proud as any man living, yet he is willing to adopt almost any substitute that will offer a change and afford an exit from his present misery.

A host of political offices have been created within the last ten years in order to provide for the new responsibility of entertaining and treating with the representatives of foreign countries. This means an increased demand for funds on the working classes. The nobility of the capital, whose names, justly or unjustly, have an ill savor in the country, are already, through this foreign influence, fallen into extravagances that the farming and tax-paying classes complain of bitterly. It is the proper thing now, especially with younger officials, to buy all that is possible of the Western world, from steamships, electric lights and gatling guns, to watches, clocks, and drawing-room ornaments. This may seem a small matter, yet it tells heavily on a people so impoverished.

Until twelve years ago, there was nothing new under the sun upon which even unscrupulous nobility could squander the nation's money; now the doors are open, and no one knows the limit to the possibility of purchase. These latter-day extravagances, together with the death of trade and manufacture, have brought the Korean subject to a desperately ominous point in his history.

It has been said by some careless observers that Korea is without a religious system. Statements to this effect have appeared so often in American papers that some reason ought to be given for this misunderstanding. Perhaps it is because Korea has no religion apart from her national life—her whole existence, from king to coolie, being one complicated system of ancestor worship—that one may so easily fail to notice what enters so subtly into every detail of her life.

There is to be found at New Year's in every household a spread of ancestral food. Even the poorest puts forth an effort to make a luxurious display in the presence of the spirits of his fathers. Fruit, rice, meats, distilled drinks, incense, candles, are some of the items on the list for ancestral worship. The natives put off their greasy garments and, dressed immaculately, sit out the night. When the first cock crows the candles are lighted before the tablet

—this tablet consisting of two walnut slabs fastened together, with an opening between where the spirit is said to reside. The worshippers bow, offer drink, and call on the shades to accept their sacrifice. Then when each in turn has made his salutation, they retire from the room and lock the door in order that the spirits may inhale the offering unembarrassed by the presence of the living. Again they circle about and bow repeatedly until the end, when they set to and feast on what the spirit leaves —a dinner that is supposed to bring them earthly prosperity, but which to all appearances leaves them disordered in stomach and poorer in pocket for many days to come.

New Year's is *the* sacrificial season, but it by no means includes all. For three years after the death of parents, night and morning the children offer food, meat, and tobacco, before the tablet in the room where the dead once lived, making besides, numerous offerings at the grave. From the palace to the lowest mud hut the three years of mourning and daily sacrifice are observed with the utmost strictness. During such time the royal household is occupied entirely with the spirits of the dead, believing that the prosperity of their dynasty hangs upon such worship. In the case of poor people, they bring their food and, staff in hand, with loud lamentations, spread it out before their father's ghost. After this period they limit the direct sacrifices to about six important days in the year—the four national fête days, and the anniversaries of birth and death. A native absent from his ancestral home, will walk from the farthest end of the peninsula, if necessary, to be at the grave at the appointed day. Such devoutness in religious service I have never seen even among the strictest Romanists, nor have I read of anything surpassing it among Mohammedans or Hindus.

As for the universality of these sacrifices I have never heard of any failure except among the handful of Buddhists and the few professing Christians. To neglect this is to make oneself an outlaw in the land of one's fathers—"dogs that ought not to live." A native called Kim went, according to custom, to pay his respects to an elder relative. The first greeting was, "You have failed of late to sacrifice!" "Yes," says Kim, "I cannot sacrifice again." "Then away with you; no relative of mine; a reprobate, that would mix with the dogs and forget his fathers." It is quite as much as a man's life is worth to neglect this sacred custom.

The time between sacrificial ceremonies is taken up with searching the hills for a propitious site for burial. In this choice there are many points to be taken into consideration. So complicated and mixed are the methods employed for arriving at a proper conclusion, that a large number of people make it a special study and gain their living as experts in geomancy. A grave is chosen on a mountain front if possible, having two arm-like ridges on either hand, one called the dragon side and one the tiger. There should be a mountain directly in the foreground called the *an-san*, to stand as a support to the family of the dead, otherwise the grave-luck would flow down the valley and be dissipated. There must be free exit for streams or surface waters. This is the grave site in outline. Then come the special mountain peaks that are looked for on either side of the *an-san*. One will mean long life to the family, another numerous posterity, another rank, another wealth. Every mountain peak to right or left hand has its special message, which the geomancer holds in his professional grasp.

After burial the native watches, as a matter of vital moment, to see that no one encroaches on, or interferes with, his ancestral graves. If it becomes a choice between feeding or clothing the living and making some outlay for this resting place of the dead, he will decide in a breath in favor of the latter. Should a household meet with repeated disaster, they exhume their ancestors' bones and bury them elsewhere, thinking thus to conciliate the spirits. From the idea of certain localities being possessed, has grown the belief that there are spirits in every mound, rock, and tree. Also, from the years of sacrifice in the home, comes the idea of a guardian spirit, which is worshipped by food, prayer, and characters posted on the walls. A species of venomous snake so commonly makes its home under the tiles, and is seen winding in and about the roofs of Korean huts, that they have associated with him this guardianship, and one of the commonest kinds of worship is prayer and offering to the serpent. To this has been added a host of other spirits, such as the guardian dragon, which they worship by dropping food into the well, his supposed retreat. In this guardianship they include weasels, swine, and unclean animals of every kind, giving to each so many days in the year, thus making a constant round of religious ceremony.

Some interested in Korea have thought that there are two religions: one cultured and refined, and understood to be ancestor worship; the other heathenish throughout, the lowest form of fetichism. Koreans themselves however make no distinction; they call it all *kwisin* worship, and *kwisin* is a word that is translated "demon" in the Chinese and Korean New Testament. They themselves claim that their worship is all of one origin, which agrees exactly with 1. Cor. x: 20, "But I say that the things which the Gentiles sacrifice they sacrifice to demons and not to God."

The land is dotted over with little temples, reared in honor of those who have been faithful to their parents, more especially after the parents' death. Near my present home, there is a tablet, erected some hundred and fifteen years ago, with this inscription, "Kim Ik Pin, a faithful son lost his father at ten years of age. His mourning was like the mourning of a man; his flesh wasted away, and his bones alone remained. At seventeen, when the season of sacrifice came round, and there was no fish to be had because of the summer rains, he went out and prayed by the seashore, weeping in agony, when lo! a fish from the water came falling at his feet. Again we see his devotion, for when fires had surrounded the mountains, threatening to envelope his father's grave and burn his spirit, in he rushed at the risk of life, praying the gods to spare his ancestor's resting place; and down came the rainy season's floods and quenched the fire. Was he not a faithful son!"

Books used everywhere in schools, and taught the children, deal exclusively with the subject of sacrifice to King, parents, elder brothers, etc. I give here a translation of a story from "The Five Social Virtues"—a book known to every one in Korea who has passed his primer. "During the Han dynasty, there lived a man called Tong Yŏng, a citizen of Chŏng sŏng district. His father died, and Yŏng having no means of giving him honorable burial borrowed ten thousand cash, agreeing to pay the debt in money or give himself as bond slave. Returning from the funeral, he was on his way to slavery, when suddenly there appeared before him a queenly lady, who requested him to take her for his wife. Yŏng, amazed, answered, 'I, so poor that I am even now on my way to bond service, why do you ask to become my wife?' The lady replied, 'I wish to be your wife, that is enough; your poverty and humble station give me no cause for shame.' Thus urged, he took her with him, and the debt-master asked if she understood any kind of handiwork. 'I can weave,' she answered. 'Then,' he replied, 'if you will weave me three hundred bales of silk, I'll give you both freedom.' This amount he knew to be more than the work of a lifetime. Within a month the three hundred bales were finished, and the master in fear, sent them quickly away. As they passed the spot again which had seen their first meeting, she said to Yŏng, 'I must leave you now; for I am a woman come from the Weaver's Star. Heaven saw your filial piety, and being moved with love, sent me to pay your debt.' Thus speaking she ascended into heaven."

It is the teaching of Confucius interpreted

and added to. The object of it all is to teach earthly prosperity as the reward of faithfulness. There has never been a time that so strongly proves this system a failure in this regard as the present, and yet they still continue to worship. Hither have their ancestral gods brought them, in spite of prayers and ceremony. The land destitute of spiritual life as of earthly prosperity, is unconsciously holding out her hands for help just now. May her mute appeal arouse our tenderest sympathy!

His Excellency Mr. Yi Pöm Chin, the present Minister of Korea to the United States, told me on March 3d, 1898, that there were ten reforms he deemed necessary for his country, and that I might make them public with his name.

No. 1. The education of the great mass of the people hitherto left in ignorance and superstition.

No. 2. The encouragement of manufactures. People are forbidden to make anything their fathers knew not of. Western manufacture will break down prejudice.

No. 3. The training of an army. Korea cannot expect to compete with the outside world in military art, but she needs forces to preserve order.

No. 4. The abolition of sinecures. Offices fill the country that are of no service but to draw salary. Away with them for the fourth reform!

No. 5. The abolition of the present class gentry. That only those in office be regarded as superiors, and their children enrolled simply as the common people.

No. 6. The granting of power according to office. "At present," says Mr. Yi, "officials are officials in name only. The very duties they are assigned to, are at the disposal of others above them, which virtually nullifies the office itself."

No. 7. The teaching of Korea Western knowledge by nations specially qualified, viz: Germany for the army, England for the navy and finance, America for steam and electricity, Russia for cavalry drill, Japan for police, and China for silk manufacture.

No. 8. Governmental reform on the basis of English and German law.

No. 9. The prohibition of white as the ordinary dress.

No. 10. The abolition of Chinese literature and the establishment of *Unmun* as the national script.

XII

SOME SPECIAL FRIENDS

H. H. Prince Eui Wha. It was my privilege while in Japan, to meet frequently with Prince Eui Wha, the second son of His Majesty, the Emperor of Korea. He had come in the autumn of 1895 on a special message from his government, and had remained since that time. It was the first occasion in the history of Korea when a prince of the imperial family had gone abroad, and his impressions of foreign life were to me a matter of very great interest. He lived for a few months in Koyama, in the city of Tokyo, surrounded by a number of his fellow countrymen. Many of these being personally interested in political movements in Korea, an atmosphere was created which was distasteful to him, so he moved away during the summer of 1896 to keep himself free from even the appearance of political entanglement.

He had learned, seemingly by intuition, to dress as a foreigner of good taste, a rare exception in Japan, with its pot hats, white cotton gloves, and spare suits.

Frequently during the summer he made his way to Yokohama, and began study in prepa-

YI PŌM CHIN (CHIN POM YE).

H. I. KOREAN MAJESTY'S MINISTER TO THE UNITED STATES.

H. H. PRINCE EUI WHA.

ration for a journey to America. One of our trips taken together in company with Mr. Loomis (a constant friend and benefactor to Koreans) was to "Great Hell," a burning hill on the shore of Lake Hakone. While Korea shows signs of volcanic formation, the fires have long since become quiescent, so that an active volcano was of interest to the Prince. We came through a clump of trees into the region of fire, and found vegetation, that a year or two before had been green and luxuriant, cooked and dry. Our pathway led directly across this heated region. By driving a stick a foot or two into the ground and withdrawing it, a steam pipe resulted that would scald the passer if he came near it. We stood at last on the central part of the crater, the Prince being perfectly cool and collected as he picked his way over the dangerous ground. Here we were within the precincts of this great power-house, that labored and shook, giving furious vent to its pressure through the openings round about. The Prince was particularly interested in a chasm, into which a foreigner was said to have fallen and lost his life a year or two before. He joined us in rolling boulders into it to hear the dull thud in the bottom of the "hell" far underneath. It was a trip that showed us Prince Eui Wha's coolness and courage and powers of endurance.

In the evening we dined at a hotel where other foreigners were present—loud talking women, and men who smoked with heads back and feet up in the air. The Prince observed that there were no special marks of civilization on the foreigners who frequented that hotel. Some time later we attended a concert given by the Choral and Philharmonic Societies of Yokohama, and the whole programme was of great interest. The Prince enjoyed the music though it was still a foreign language to him. His only adverse criticism reminded me of a story of President Lincoln, who remarked of one of Mrs. Lincoln's evening dresses, that it would look better with a piece of the tail cut off and put round the neck. Oriental civilization is quite as much characterized by common sense and good judgment as is our own.

The Prince learned while in Japan to ride a wheel, and after an hour or so of study each day, we would have a run over the drives about Yokohama. The Japanese policeman who accompanied him in a 'riksha, would have to be reinforced two or three times in order to keep within sight of the wheel. It was one of the pleasures the Prince enjoyed in his quiet way, to see how many knots an hour he could get out of 'riksha coolies.

I have also seen much of the Prince during his stay in America, and have accompanied him frequently through the turmoil of these great cities. American life to him is unlovely and associated with much unpleasantness. This is not due to lack of courtesy in the American people, but to antagonistic parties at home who have succeeded in leaving him stranded. His condition of humiliation has proven more clearly than prosperity could, the high-bred aristocracy from which he is descended. Without complaint or threat, he has borne patiently an exile's life in a distant land. I am convinced of his worth apart altogether from the position that comes to him by inheritance. A neatly dressed, modest young man, seen passing frequently along Twelfth Street, Washington, is the second son of the emperor of Korea, though his surroundings and position betoken nothing imperial.

I have heard of princes in disguise that lived long ago in fairy tales, of which stories a peculiar fulfillment is experienced, when I find myself introducing one as plain Mr. Yi, who is a prince of the Hermit Kingdom, the last remnant of the fairylands of antiquity.

Through these little incidents of each day, and through the quiet hours of study, we have learned to see the manliness, courage and true nobility of this son of the emperor. His ideas of, and desires for life, are of the highest type. We trust and pray that he may be so guided, that he will yet be a blessing to his country, and we take the liberty of marking him as one of our special friends, in whom we are particularly interested, and for whom we have the highest admiration.

Don Quixote. My unfortunate friend Kang had something in his face and manner that reminded me of the name by which I head this paragraph. So I learned to think of him, and so I always called him. One of his first remarks to me was that we were near the last days, and that it was about all up with the Land of Morning Calm. I first met Don Quixote in a Buddhist temple down south. Our friendship grew rapidly, to such an extent that he sent me three live hens and fifty eggs. I would have appreciated the gift more had not those hens been so hard to entertain. My boy, in a murderous way, managed to tether them by strings in a corner of the yard. While they lived, their lives were a confused struggle; and when they died, their cries threw a shadow over my soul. I felt at the time as though it argued unfavorably for my friendship with the Don.

The old man told me that he was proprietor of a steamship he had bought from a Japanese pirate. I had heard a shrill whistling along the coast a few days before, which was thus explained. The steamer was about the size of a canal-tug, with a long slim smokestack above deck, and a short thick-set Japanese below, who was in charge of the engine. She scarcely looked seaworthy, so I asked the Don how far he had been in his ship. Said he "What's that big port in Mi-guk?" (America). "San Francisco?" I asked. "So, so," says he, "Sang Prisko. I've been to Sang Prisko." The Don is older than I, so it was not proper for me to contradict or to tell him that he must be mistaken, that he and his matchbox would have been down with Davy Jones long before they reached "Sang Prisko."

The Don often came to see me, drank tea and smoked his long pipe. One day he began conversation in this way "Brother, you are known all over the world, and so am I." "No! no!" I said, "I'm not known at all except to one or two old friends who have not forgotten me." He would not believe this, and went on to say that he had two proposals to make and would come the next day to lay them before me. The next day came and the Don likewise, aglow with his proposals. Said he, "One is this, that you come with me and be manager of my ship, and we will be traders; and seeing that the world knows us she will give us what we ask." I thanked him but said that I was not a navigator, so could never run his ship; that it took all the skill I had to steer my way on land. He seemed very much cut up, and said that I was not unable but unwilling. Then he came with his second proposal, took hold of my hand and spoke in a whisper. "I'll take a knife and open a vein in my wrist, and you open one in yours. We'll mix the blood and be one forever. If you die, I'll die with you, and if I die, you'll die with me." "Yes! let me see, I'm afraid I can't do that either." "Why?" he asked. "That might not be best, I might give you bad blood out of my veins." "I'll risk it," said the Don. I reasoned with him, and asked if we could not be friends without this. After a long talk he concluded that it was not possible, wrote with his finger the character "shin," meaning "trust," which along with a shake of the head, meant there was no faith without the blood, and so we parted.

Months passed. I moved back to the capital and took up my home in a little Korean room in a crowded part of the city. One evening, in the dusk, returning by the great South Gateway, I heard some one call from the crowd "Keui-li! Keui-li!" I turned and it was Don Quixote—poor old Don! He looked hard up, his face more cadaverous than ever, his coat faded and soiled. I asked, with surprise, "Why, how do you happen to be here? Is it peace?" "Peace," he replied, and then said he had lost his ship, was out of money, cold and nearly starving. Would he not come round and have something to eat? He said "Not now, some other day," and disappeared. Filled with sadness I returned, leaving him to wend his uncertain way "whitherward"—which way it seems was to the Hyöng-jo or national prison where, under the shadow of the sabre, and awaiting his sentence for debt, and I know not what all, Don Quixote disappeared from view. There I had to leave him to rough through alone what remained of life. The bastinado, or what is often preferred to it, the turf outside the East Gate with its sword and executioner, are old, old stories in Chosön. Multitudes have marched by way of these to the eternity that awaits us all. Fare thee well! poor old Don! a longer journey it was than across the sea to Mi-guk. He thought to fight great armies single-handed and he failed.

Old Kim. We had gone northeast to plant a Christian mission on the coast of Korea. We found a house, and then announced to this strange people the object of our coming. On the first day of meeting the room was filled, and in the farthest corner sat a little oldish man, with face afire, listening while I read. At the close he stood and made an address of his own. "This doctrine," said he, "tells a man to hate his father and mother, and marry his brother's wife. Wrong? Of course! Away with it! Everybody knows it is wrong," and he left indignant. But he came again, and the fiery face grew pinched with listening. He drank in the words: "Rest for the wanderer; bread for the hungry; all who are troubled, come! And the man that was dead heard His voice; and the poor outcast woman found that He cared for her; and the thief, who deserved to die, was taken home to heaven; and He Himself suffered with His hands nailed through and His feet torn and His garments bedraggled with blood." The tears had come, and old Kim was on his feet. With tenderness in his voice he told the people that he did not know how or why, but the story of Jesus was for him. He trusted that his heart was at peace with God, the first time in fifty years. There was a great consternation among the people. Kim's face was changed, the look of woe was gone and an expression of peace was written upon it. He went to the elders of the village and told them what had been done for him. They were all upset, and the town was in confusion, for Kim prayed so loud at night that he terrified the people. They in turn offered sacrifice, and cried to their gods to save the town from the spirit that had entered it. One bolder than others, defied God, threatened Kim, and blasphemed in his poor, ignorant way, and then left for his home underneath the hills. But a great rain came, and a part of the hill slid off and buried the man; then Kim prayed that God would save the people and stop the landslides. Gradually from a wicked man, Kim became what all the townsfolk called a good man, though a little crazy, and they nicknamed him *Chöm Yüng Kam* (Little Old Man). Little he was in the eyes of his countrymen, and older than his age, for he lived not here, but beyond the eternities in the life to come.

Only a year remained, and it was a hard year of suffering. "Once," said he, "I was cutting grass for fuel, and the weariness was so great that I knelt down among the reeds to tell Him of it; then He gave me such peace and such indescribable delight. Oh! If the people only knew it, they would all believe in Him." But we had no suitable meeting house in which the people could gather to hear, and the times were very hard. I told Kim I feared it was out of the question, but he rebuked me saying, "Brother! who runs this world?" and with that he went to the end of the veranda and prayed and shouted so loud, that all the people in the town could hear him. He wanted a meeting-house in which to preach the good news, and he thanked God for the promise of answer. The meeting house is built now, but Kim never saw it, for his body was already sleeping in the dust awaiting the resurrection.

To the last he was faithful, and when life was nearly ended and strength gone, he gave us who were left strength and encouragement. Death and resurrection! The wisest seek in vain by wisdom to find out what they are, and have to give up the search and die forgotten; while a poor old heathen, who has never known anything, finds the secret and dies triumphantly.

On a sunny slope among the pines, near his little mud cabin, there is a green mound that marks his grave. We knew him less than two years; and after all he was only a poor backwoods Korean, but his going meant loneliness to us and his memory brings the tears.

Auntie. Among the women of Korea, I have one old friend who sometimes does mending, and as the women have no name given them I call her Auntie. I asked Auntie why it was they made such prisoners of the women. She said, "It's custom, you know, custom (p'ung-sok), and you can't change custom." Auntie is sixty-three now, but she still wears a mantle as she walks the streets in remembrance of girlhood days. She says, "I belonged to the working class, you know. When I was quite young a *yangban* (nobleman) brought me from the country to be his slave, and I never saw my home again. After some years I was married, but my husband died when I was only thirty-four, and since then I've had to work hard to live." This is Auntie's history as she gives it. To judge from the white hair and deeply furrowed face, I would say that if it were all told, it would be a longer and more toilsome history than this.

Auntie says she would not mind it all, if it were not for a sickness that she has had these ten summers now, " a breathing sickness " she calls it; something that catches her at the corners of the breath, and she adds, " When the breath won't go, nothing goes." She has been to see the magicians and medicine men and lastly the prophets, but it is all in vain. "They are very wise and very great," she says, "but they can't make breath."

The Abbot of Sök-wang-sa.

Um-söl-ha is the abbot of Sök-wang-sa. He is a man of ponderous physique, and yet the mortal part of him is insufficient to lodge the soul, for he gasps and wheezes and pants from internal pressure. He is between seventy and eighty years of age, and so heavy are all his alignments, that his eyes have scarcely lifted their lids for a quarter of a century. Though a man of peace, he has the voice of a bloodhound; and though born son of the Buddha, he has the expression and countenance of an eighty-ton gun. Mass, weight, and volcanic pressure attend him in this life; while a *nirvana* of material nothingness awaits him in the world to come.

Once after twenty miles across the plains, hot and malarial with rice fields, we entered the shady avenues of the monastery, and passed the gateway into the outer guest chamber. Priests and monks welcomed us, and a moment later the abbot himself squeezed his way through the narrow door, and in a voice of distant thunder said, "Peace!" He lifted his eyes, and looked long and inquiringly at the strangers. Could our honorable stomachs, he asked, tolerate the fare of his humble abbey? We replied that our depraved digestion would be delighted to refresh itself on the viands of His Holiness' table; and thus the necessary formalities being completed, we were left to converse freely. The doctrine we brought was of special interest. Was it like that of Buddha? And did we pray in Sanscrit and Pali, "*Suri suri su suri saba*," just as he did, and they did in China and Anam and India? He called the monks in to hear what we had to say, and maintained that a doctrine so simple and plain as ours ought to do every one good. We were interrupted by the piping of a mosquito that circled about, seeking some one to devour.

BUDDHIST MONKS.

BUDDHIST PAGODA.

The abbot motioned to a monk not to kill it, but to shoo it from the room, as you would a chicken, careful to take no life for the glory of the Buddha.

Our evening meal of rice, pressed seaweed, and roots was over, and then we sat and read from the Gospel till late into the night; all the monks listening, questioning and repeating, till the abbot reminded us that it was late and they must let us rest from our journey. He pointed me to an inscription on the wall, a charm he said against biters, bugs, and unclean insects of every kind, so, "rest ye in peace."

It was after midnight, and I had just dozed off when the drums of the monastery, big and little, awoke, each answering to the other, slow and loud at first, but with dwindled flutterings at the end. Then all the monks began in consonance of prayer: "*Namu Amit'abul! Namu Amit'abul!*" (I put my trust in Buddha! I put my trust in Buddha!). I looked through the chink of the doorway, and there they were with faces to the stone floor, repeating with all the "go" of a steam praying-wheel, faster and faster, "I believe in Buddha, I believe in Buddha"— while the brass-faced god leered at its worshippers in the dim monastic twilight. Through the sounds of worship came the rich sonorous voice of the chief of all the monastery, "I believe in Buddha, I believe in Buddha." Seventy years of searchings had brought him no answer, nothing but the leering face of his loudly painted god. Then the worship ended with bells of different tones, soft and silvery, and once more gods and men slept.

A week after my return home, two monks came with a present of wooden bowls from the abbot—bowls that he himself had used on his table for years—and would I accept them in remembrance of an old priest whose soul was soon to transmigrate? He also wished the monks to stay and learn of the Jesus Buddha, whom I had said was greater than Sökamoni.

But a question came into the abbot's life. One day a Westerner, who claimed to be a follower of Jesus, alighted at the monastery, brass-faced and iron-fisted. He poked the Buddha with a club, told all the monks that they were destined to outer darkness, and when the grey-haired abbot sat by dignified and respectful, caught him by the back of the neck, and chucking his head to the floor said, "Bow to the image, you old heathen, bow!" In the abbot's mind Sökamoni was after all more to be desired than this Jesus Buddha.

On a hot sultry day, with staff in hand, the abbot walked twenty miles to pay me a call and inquire concerning these things. He admitted that his Buddha had not answered the questionings of his heart. There was still a dark interrogation mark on his soul. But he said that sometimes he almost arrived at peace, when he beat the drums, rang the bells, and said one hundred and eight times, "I believe in Buddha, I believe in Buddha." And how could Jesus be good; for there was this man with the club and the iron fist? I told him that Jesus could satisfy; that the mischief was with us, His followers, not with Him. The abbot's eyes are not large, but they have seen into life for a space of seventy years, and they are not to be deceived by a sham of godliness.

One request he had, would I show him the house we lived in; and my wife and family being absent, I took him through alone. The pictures on the walls—did we worship them? A small harmonium he thought would be an admirable charm to wake the Buddha. And then the books with the strange letters written in them—and a mirror or two—and the beautiful glass windows—and such fine dishes we ate out of—and chairs and curtains—all beautiful as *nirvana*. When we were through, I asked the abbot what he would like best of all he saw. "Preserve me from covetousness," said he, "but the glass dish in the 'wall box,' with the crystal cover and a knob on the top like a jewel in the lotus." "It is yours," I said, "only a very humble present that cost me nothing." The abbot took his departure, his monk carrying a New Testament for him, and his precious preserve dish "clear as crystal."

XIII

A MISSIONARY CHAPTER

We imagine in our home land that the word heathen is a synonym for all that is evil and detestable in human nature, but this conception is very far from the truth. If you want the worst people in the world you will find them in America—in Sing-Sing, and out of Sing-Sing. The Gospel is a savor of death unto death, quite as much as it is a savor of life unto life. Where it is preached you will find the greatest evil as well as the greatest good.

We believe that Korea merits quite as much as does India, what Max Müller says regarding the truthful character of the Hindus. In some respects a lack of truth is seen, as I mentioned in the chapter on the Korean mind; but we have to specify, for at the next turning there may be discovered just as striking an example of the presence of this very virtue. I have been impressed by the quiet simple life of the people of Korea—especially in the village communities—heathen idolaters though they be. Their hospitality is a most striking characteristic. There are no beggars, except about foreign settlements. A hungry wayfarer needs but to step into the guest-room of a gentleman's home, and he will be fed and cared for for nothing. A traveller, if he have no air of suspicion about him, may journey from end to end of the peninsula without money, confident that there is hospitality awaiting him at every turning.

The simple, patriarchal style of life is more conducive to honesty than our complicated systems. If you go with me to a farmhouse you will see how country people live. There is the field where they grow the cotton. There, in a room in the inner inclosure of the house, the women spin and weave it into dress goods. For extras, the silk worms are busy feeding on mulberry leaves and winding their cocoons. These too are taken, spun, and woven; and so in the compass of one home you find your dress materials. The black hats and head-bands are usually bought, though the wide straw shades are woven by the men. Straw shoes too are made by any male member of the family. A Korean can accomplish marvels with a bundle of loose straw. He makes from what we would throw away as useless, shoes, ropes, and mats— all beautifully woven. Then there are the fields of rice and buckwheat. The rice is gathered in sheaves, and threshed out over a log before the door, the grain falling on mats. This again is hulled by a water pestle or large hammer, worked by a running stream. The grain is put into a hollowed stone, and the hammer pounds away until all is hulled. Then it is ground by two women at the mill, one turning the stone and the other feeding the grain. Here is their food and clothing. Little is left for them to buy, so they require but little money.

In some respects Koreans are exceedingly trustworthy; more so than we are in our enlightened land. I once knew an American lady who lived alone with two little children in the capital. She was quite unprotected by bolts or gates, and had plenty in her home to tempt the natives. Being aware of this we had one of the coolies of the street to sleep every night just before the stove by her bedroom door. Through the anxious hours he was there rolled up in his blanket, a bundle of unkemptness, but faithful as a collie dog; and had it been necessary he would have died for her.

Once on the east coast I was in need of money and telegraphed for one hundred dollars by special courier. This was Thursday night, and the distance from the capital was one hundred and eighty miles. On Monday morning at breakfast, a mud-bespattered coolie announced himself, and handed me wrapped in paper one hundred dollars. He had made nearly sixty miles a day over the roughest roads in Korea to bring me the money safely. He was not worth a dollar himself, and a hundred would have kept him for years. Why did he not run off or say he had been robbed? Because he was too much of a man, was to be trusted, and had a sense of honor.

The natives, too, are orderly. Markets and other gatherings scarcely require police as ours do. They have a sense of fairness that enters into business relations. Business credit stands as high with them as with us, and a man's word in a bargain is taken for more than it is in America. If you pay for land, the public will stand by you in possession of it whether you have a deed or not.

Another remarkable fact is the trustworthiness of house servants. Money and valuables can be left in their care with perfect safety. Year after year will pass with not once a dishonest act. This has been the experience of more than one foreigner. Some hold that it is from fear of punishment that they do not fall into sin, but fear never yet kept a man long straight in anything. Fear would wear off, and their real character come to the surface, in less time than we have given them for a testing.

For eight years I had in my employ a young man who had been born with some means, and so had not learned to work. He had spent his life at school in the study of Chinese. I first met him in a little hut on the seashore many miles from the capital. He had an attractive manner that took my fancy, and I asked him if he would come with me. He agreed, and we made our first visit to Fusan together. Other natives had warned me against him, as being easily led into bad company, which was true, in a way; but notwithstanding this defect, in all the eight years never once did he deceive or fail me. He was ever ready to sacrifice his own comfort or convenience to mine; would give extras from his table in his desire that I should fare well; would lay his few treasures, whatever they might be, at my feet, if he thought they could be of use; was insulted and abused for standing for my honor—and yet, faithful in everything for eight long years, as far as his relationship to me and those around me was concerned, his was the most faultless life I have ever seen.

By nature Koreans are quite as good as we—better, I think. They need no Western schooling or higher education to prepare them for the Gospel. They are prepared already, and are worthy of the best that we can give them. Not that they are without faults, but these excellencies they have, and more, for as a rule they are good to their wives, and kind to their children;

but in the spiritual world they are all wrong, and here we discover the marks of heathenism.

Their **huts are** the dwelling places of idolatry. They worship various spirits **or** gods in each room, one for the kitchen, one for the outer chamber, etc. Most of this fetichism is sanctioned by the men and carried on by the women. They throw rice into the well to quiet the dragon, and offer sacrifice to *Ma-ma*, the god of smallpox and to other unclean spirits. They worship snakes, **weasels, and pigs,** and not a day goes by but the spirit of some animal must be propitiated. The sounds that **awake you** at night are most of them connected with heathen worship. "Aigo! Aigo! Aigo!" means that some one is dead and they are sitting in sackcloth and ashes wailing thus. A gong that has a peculiar tin-pan tone to it, has often disturbed me. It is meant as a kind of solace or requiem to the soul on its journey to the other land. Once a friend of mine **was** dying, and as soon as it became **known** to **the** natives, **an** old woman **or two** came with gongs and sat outside the yard enclosure beating them till he passed away. A peculiar **weird** shriek, heard night and day in the streets of the capital, is from a fortune-teller or prophet **who** finds abundance of people to employ him. Along **the roadway** there are devil-posts cut with grinning teeth, and **planted there to** keep malignant spirits from passing. When cholera broke out in 1895, we had them all about us with an inscription written along the front, "This is the general who is after the cholera devils." Besides this a ditch would be dug across the roadway to make sure that no spirit should pass.

Another mark of heathenism is the idea that the exposure of decapitated bodies will serve as a preventative of evil doing. One day when riding past the execution ground beyond the East Gate, I saw a number of human heads on the roadway, trampled by the horses, the grass about bespattered with blood, and a little further on were the bodies with the ravens feeding on them. The people going by wagged their heads like the Jews past Golgotha. A soldier on the field of battle dies honorably, but the ghastliness of an execution ground is beyond words to express; and yet to this our Saviour came in His humiliation and suffering.

One cold day on a trip into the country, I was ahead of the horses walking to keep warm, when I came upon a mat by the roadside from beneath which I saw hands and feet protruding. I asked my boy what this was, and he said, "A dead Korean. Very cold you know, sir!" He was left right under two great gods cut out of the mountain side, that watched me all the afternoon; but the gods were immovable—and

A Missionary Chapter

the frozen man was immovable—and the people were immovable as the stony-hearted gods they worship.

Long journeys fall to the lot of the missionary, and on these he has ample opportunity for studying the character of the people. There are streams to be forded, little hovels to sleep in, vermin and disease to contend with, and all the varnish is worn off of life, and people go about in their true color, but you never find a horse-boy who is not willing to take you on his back over the fiercest torrent, if only his legs are long enough to fathom it. One chilly day we reached a boiling stream with a stony bottom, that went right across the roadway. My long thin *mapu* (horse-boy) rolled up his pantaloons and took me on his back, for the horse had all it could do to make his own way over. Step by step he entered the *sturm und drang*, and then just midway, everything collapsed, and I was pitched into the cold watery confusion. The poor boy apologized again and again. He really had not felt so much shame since his father died. I was not so cold or wet but what I could appreciate the honest look of dejection in his face.

Their speech too bears upon it the mark of the beast, for there are two different languages, where one easy one might serve. One is the written or eye-language, and the other is the spoken or ear-language. No one understands the eye-language when it is read, and no one thinks of writing the ear-language as it is spoken. When you make a note of what is said, you have to translate it from the ear-language into the eye-language; and when you read from a book to listeners, you have to translate from the eye-language into the ear-language. The languages in their character and construction differ as widely as English differs from Syriac; for they belong to different families and are in no sense related whatever. The ear-language, which all the people understand, is considered beneath the dignity of the scholar and official class to use as a means of written communication, so they spend twenty years on the study of the eye-language, and then most of them fail to use it successfully. No more hopeless confusion exists than in the use of the original languages in Korea. From this confusion we are hoping to bring forth a Christian literature that will be understood and appreciated by the mass of the people.

No sooner do the people learn that we are there to teach Christianity than they come from all quarters, and from all sorts of motives— some for rice, some for work, some for money and some again to be freed from devils and evil spirits. None of course come from a desire for Christianity, unless they have heard of it from others, for a man cannot very well desire what he knows nothing about. Many who have been beset by evil influences, come in great terror and ask some way of deliverance. Our remedy is to read from the New Testament, translating the English into Korean as we proceed. They listen with eagerness, and I have seen those who were in bondage transformed entirely while dwelling on these stories from the Gospel. As a result their homes have become cleaner and tidier, the idols and other objects of worship have disappeared, and you could feel that it was true, when they said they had experienced a great deliverance.

Among the inquirers special ones seem to be sent. One Pak came in fear to know of salvation. We read to him, taught him, and he came the next day intensely in earnest: the day following he was gone with cholera.

There was a poor worthless coolie by the name of Shin, who first called on us one morning when we were busy. My writers, who consider themselves gentlemen, insisted on putting him out of the room because he was so dirty and carried so foul an odor. Shin knew that his company was not appreciated, and when he came afterward he sat in the farthest corner to listen. A few months later, a well-dressed man with clean hands and a pure heart, sat among the Christians, and showed in his every feature what a change had been wrought in him. He had been a good-for-nothing slave to sin for years. He was in the inner prison, his feet fast in the stocks. The forces of evil were on guard about him, and the prison doors were shut. He was asleep, unconscious of the sentence of death, till the angel of the Lord came and awoke him, and said, "Follow me." And he, not knowing what he did, followed, and the irons fell off, and the keepers were powerless, and the prison doors opened, and out into the great city he went, a free man. Shin's wife took cholera and the Christians gathered for prayer. Some of them maintained that no Christian would be taken, but she grew worse and worse. When we saw her, her face wore a deathly pallor, and her poor hands were livid. She had entered the stage of collapse, and it was only a matter of a few minutes. But their prayers were answered, and she lived.

Korea we believe is worthy even of the brave comrades that have joined the noble army of martyrs, and have laid down their lives for her. The first was in the far South. While living there we received word from J. H. Davies, who had come from Australia, that he desired to make a journey to Fusan, and perhaps settle permanently. He left the capital in April, and came by way of Ch'ung ch'ŏng and Chŏlla provinces. It was a hard journey, especially for one unacclimated and but slightly acquainted with the language. The natives had misunderstood him, and had treated him in an unfriendly way. For three or four days before reaching Fusan he had been ill, but what was the matter he did not know. A card was brought me by a coolie one rainy afternoon, on which was written, "Come at once! J. H. Davies." I found him in a hut about a mile from my room. He was tanned and travel-worn, but otherwise did not look particularly ill. The coolies were pestering him for extra pay, and he asked to be defended from them. The pay was settled, and he walked, leaning on my arm, until he reached my room, where he lay on the cot resting. "I'll be well now," said he, as he tried to eat some food. I called in a Japanese physician. After an examination, disclosing marks on his body, he pronounced it smallpox. We watched all night, Mr. Yi and I. When I returned after Yi's watch, Mr. Davies said, "He was so kind to me, he bathed my brow and helped me to bear the suffering." Toward noon the next day symptoms of pneumonia set in, and the Japanese doctor, who spoke German, said, "Er wird bald sterben," which was true, for he passed away in less than an hour.

On a lonely hillside, in that far distant land, with only a dusky native or two to help me, I buried all that was left of J. H. Davies, a brave, true-hearted Christian, who gave his life for Korea.

It was only a few weeks later that two of my friends came overland, Mr. Fenwick and Dr. J. W. Heron, physician at that time to the various legations, and to His Majesty the king. After a stay of a day or two, the latter insisted on my returning with him by steamer to Seoul, as I stood in need of a change. Not long after reaching the capital we made a trip to Nam Han, to arrange a summer resort, to tide the foreigners over the hot season. We made a circuit of the walls one forenoon, picked flowers, and examined points of interest. There was in my friend's mind that morning the prospect of a visit home; and many things spoken as commonplace then, have a peculiar deep meaning now. The walk had been recreation; he must mount horse and get back to the city hospital, with its crowds of diseased and crippled waiting for his coming. Many a native, from the king to the poorest coolie, had found relief from bodily suffering under his skillful hand. He was a knight of Christian chivalry and his surgeon's lance was the weapon he wielded. None of his own people was forgotten either in his labors for the natives, for he felt that he was entrusted with their lives and safety too. How well he watched and guarded! Brave, fearless brother! who commanded the respect of the highest, and the hearts and affections of the lowest. His unselfish, kindly way, was the spiritual sermon that always accompanied his daily labors. But a week later he was down with a fell disease, and the one who had so often ministered to the sick was destined to go. A day or two of suffering, and a few of us watched by him as his spirit passed quietly away, without a ripple. His last words were to his soldier and native friends who gathered around him as retainers about their chief. "Jesus," said he, "loves you. He gave His life for you. Stand by Him!" The sleep was given that marked him as one beloved, and his body was laid to rest on the banks of the river Han. He stood among the noblest and best of men, and he laid down his life for the people of Korea.

It was not long till we were called upon to mourn the loss of another physician, Dr. Hall, who came out under the Methodist Board, and whose presence in Korea had been a benediction to us all. He too was of the sainted type that we meet but seldom in Christian experience. The great masters could not begin to picture the Saviour's face as truly as it was pictured in the face of Brother Hall. He so reflected that glory that I for one, at least, felt an increased sense of guilt and sin in his presence.

It fell to Dr. Hall to open P'yöng-yang along

with Mr. Moffett. P'yöng-yang had up till the time of the war been a stronghold of evil, and Dr. Hall lived in the worst part of the city. In my own mind I have pictured him through the times of persecution and trial, patient and long-suffering, letting his light shine just as the Saviour did, often spending the time that health required in the sunlight, in a dark little room praying and supplicating God that He would open P'yöng-yang city to the Saviour. The city is now open, and the dear brother's prayers are answered; but he himself is absent from us, and we say,

> "Oh for the touch of a vanished hand,
> And the sound of a voice that is still."

He, too, sleeps beside his comrade, Dr. Heron, on the banks of the river Han: another who gave his life for the people of Korea.

The Korean is by nature a hero-worshipper. He loves a giant six feet three or four, with broad back and thick hand, who can play pitch and toss with the sorrows and burdens of life. This accounts for their admiration of missionary McKenzie from his first arrival. I have so often heard in connection with him that he was *chey-il* (number one), in everything. Nobody so tall, or stout, or strong as he. He had a giant's voice, they said, and yet his Christlikeness made him gentle as a lamb. He was universally beloved. I have heard it repeated that nobody believed like Kim Moksa (McKenzie). He was to them the embodiment of Christian strength and courage. When the Tonghaks came down with murder and pillage, all the natives ran but Kim Moksa (McKenzie), not he. He was like a rock planted deep, that nothing could move. So the Christians brought their goods to him to keep. And when war was going on, timid ones gathered under the flag with a red cross that floated over the hut where he lived alone with his native friends. Murderers, with swords red with blood, who came down to kill the "foreign devil," skulked away like dogs, afraid of one who looked to them the lion of the Tribe of Judah. He not only raised up a Christian community, but he taught the boys to play ball, and to make men of themselves physically, as well as spiritually. He was the light of the seacoast of Western Whang-hă. But when he had borne witness through the time of trial, and had carried his brethren safely in his arms, his work was done. Disease that is stronger than the giant, fastened upon him. He suffered as a brave martyr, tasting in his death a humiliation, that to my mind made him more like his Saviour, for in an hour of unconsciousness, he shot himself. The natives were heart-broken at this trial of their faith; but they buried him, kindly and lovingly, underneath the trees on the seashore, where he had borne his witness and lived so bravely for his Master.

There is still another of precious memory, whom we include in this martyr band, Dr. H. M. Brown, whose quick temper and warm heart breathed of the Highlands of Scotland. We remember Dr. Brown more for the kindness of his nature than for anything else. He was the embodiment of that Christian love and charity which fights against great odds, and conquers. He too, like his brother of the Highlands, McKenzie, was a man of powerful physique, and when at last he had to lay down his arms and surrender, it was like the surrender of Napoleon. While on the field he made rapid progress in the language, and even when an invalid, was building, studying, and teaching, as though he had been well. But consumption had gained its hold, and it was only a matter of time with him, though his heart kept up and his courage was firm. There was an honesty and openness of character that was beautiful. Every thought was expressed, every conviction of his soul he stood by. This very honesty was the cause of his greatest mistakes. If he saw one downtrodden his Highland blood was up. One day while walking with him in the streets of the capital, we passed a group of men and boys intent on a cockfight. The birds were covered with blood and nearly exhausted. Quick as thought, Brown caught one under his arm, and marched straight ahead with a howling mob after him ordering him to drop it. One man caught him by the shoulder and meant to take the bird by force, when the doctor by a simple twist so reversed the man's ideas that he walked nimbly away. He intended to save the creature if possible, so when he reached a high enclosure he threw it over to the other side, and it disappeared among the roofs. His teacher too fell a victim to a most unjust charge and was locked up in the *yamen* to be beaten and maltreated under name of the law. Brown took the situation in in a flash, and in just about the style Sir William Wallace would have done it, broke open that *yamen* gate and set his teacher free. Meanwhile the governor and his soldiers were looking on meekly from a safe distance in the rear. It was a mistake, yet I admire the man that it showed him to be, don't you? He was a Christian soldier, full of the spirit of chivalry. He never fought for self or for a selfish purpose, but for principle and for the rights of others. When his strong hand could fight no more, he lay down to his rest, in the conviction that his Lord was coming to set poor downtrodden, imprisoned, mortals free.

Korea has cost us already the bravest and best that we had, and all in the short space of twelve years. But there are now over a thousand Christians, whereas after the same time in Japan there were only ten, while in China they worked nearly forty years for ten. Thus Korea in making her returns is showing that it was not in vain that these brave men died.

www.ingramcontent.com/pod-product-compliance
Lightning Source LLC
Chambersburg PA
CBHW031944230426
43672CB00010B/2043